Understanding the Kingdom of God and His Glory

Jo Ann Josey

Understanding the Kingdom of God and His Glory
Copyright © 2012 by Warehouse Ministries International

All rights reserved. No part of this book may be reproduced or transmitted in any form or by any means without written permission from the author.

ISBN 978-0985081027

Printed in USA by The Warehouse

Dedication

To all my friends and family who have so encouraged me to write this book for the body of Christ.
My parents Fred and Dell Windham and my brother Fred, Jr., thank you for not understanding but supporting me anyway.
Heather and Nikkii Nichols and Cooper Rohrbeck that think their grandmother is the greatest and tell her so often. My children Bryan Nichols and Suzii Rohrbeck that still haven't figured out exactly what it is that their mother does but do not criticize.
Rebecca Lynn King, Judy Whitener, Jan Hicks, Delta Meaux, Donna Baron, Durleen Williams, David and Kathie Walters and Theron Sealock, God could not have given me a greater set of cheerleaders in my corner. You mean a lot to me. Elizabeth Judd and Rosemary Gates I have loved watching you both grow. My Aunt Imogene Ball thanks for your encouragement and the thrill of watching you not only grasp the Kingdom but teach others to do the same. My Aunt Loach who is in her 90's but lights up with hunger and enthusiasm when you talk about the Kingdom of God.
Dr. Don Colbert, thank you for beleiving in me. If you are my friend and I did not mention your name it is not because you are not important to me I just can't remember every name right now but know you are loved and appreciated.

This book is for you.

Table of Contents

Introduction 5
Putting it Simply.. 7
Characteristics of the Kingdom 53
The Kingdom of God is Like.................................. 58
Gates/Doors/Courts/Throne................................. 64
The King and His Kingdom................................... 68
Territory 73
Social Order of the Kingdom 75
Diplomatic Corps – Ambassadors.......................... 88
Influence 91
Commonwealth... 94
Kingdom Economic System................................... 96
Kingdom Culture... 99
Administrative Services...................................... 106
Constitution/Covenants/Commandments/
Laws/Decrees... 109
Enemy... 113
Legal Ground.. 116
Army 117
Faith.. 119
Keys 132
Treason... 135
Ruling the Visible from the Invisible 145
The Glory of God 153

Introduction

I want to first explain to you how this book is written and why.

For those who know me, you know that I am a person who likes to get to the point. I do not like fluff or a lot of added nonsense that has nothing to do with the subject or making the point. I will leave a church service when the person in charge drags a 10 minute sermon into 50 to 80 minutes. I want to scream out "We got it the first time".

I have many teachers, that I love to listen to, who have written many books, but in the editing of the book it no longer sounds like them. I can take the first one or two sentences of a chapter and get the point. I love to listen to them but I can not read their books. "They" get lost in the editing trying to make it in correct structure and right punctuation, etc. It loses who they are and soon does not even sound like them.

When you read this book "it is me". All the sentence structure may not be correct, but "it is me". All the punctuation may not be correct and I may not use all the commas, colons, semi-colons, periods and my paragraphs maybe too long or too short, but "it is me". If these things bother you email me the mistakes you think I have made and I will correct them before the next printing, as long as they do not change who "I am".

That being said, let me explain to you that I have written this book under the inspiration of Holy Spirit and I am placing it in a two-part format. The first is for people like me and that will be called simply "Putting it Simply". The rest of the book is like a study guide broken down in chapters with all the scriptures added in. I hate to have to go to another source to look up scripture when I am reading. This will also allow you to use this book as a study guide for teaching.

I use the title "Understanding" because you can have all the wisdom and knowledge in the world but without the understanding it is of no effect in your life. All that being said, "let's get started" on the road to further "Understanding the Kingdom of God and His Glory"

"Putting it Simply"

I write this to the body of Christ under the inspiration of the Holy Spirit. It is not my opinion, but is based purely on the Word of God. In the Kingdom of God there is no place for my opinion or yours, for God only honors His Word.

The purpose of this book is to bring a revelation to the body of Christ concerning the Kingdom of which you are a part. The Kingdom has been something that, before now, only a few have had the revelation and understand of. I will endeavor to teach you how the Kingdom functions. In studying the Word, I discovered that the most important thing in the eyes of God for us is the Kingdom of God.

> But seek ye first the kingdom of God, and his righteousness; and all these things shall be added unto you.
>
> Matthew 6:33

I put things in the order of importance; therefore, if I say first, that is the thing I consider to be of greatest importance. I am created in His image and likeness, so that must also be the way God does things. This is confirmed in the fact that the only message Jesus preached was the message of the Kingdom. Further confirmed by the Scriptures is the fact that the end will not come until "the gospel of the kingdom" is preached.

If God is holding back the end of the age and the return of Jesus to the earth until the "gospel of the Kingdom" is preached to all nations, then it is indeed the most important message. The question is, then, "Why do we hear everything else preached except the Kingdom?" I think the answer is very simple; there is a lack of revelation and a lack of understanding of the Kingdom of God.

Putting it very simply, the Kingdom of God is God's chosen method of government or legal system.

I pray that this book will bring you closer to that revelation. My prayer is that you not only learn but begin to move in the revelation you receive. All the knowledge in the world is of no benefit to you unless you use it.

The Kingdom of God is made up of the following positions and departments. I am presenting to you the list of things that I have discovered as of this writing. There are probably more, and I will write of them as the Holy Spirit reveals them to me. I will briefly address each one in this section.

The Kingdom of God has these characteristics: Structure, Doors/Gates, a King, Territory, Social Order, Religion, Prayer/Communication, Diplomatic Corps, Authority, Influence, Commonwealth, Economic System, Culture, Educational System, Language, Administrative Services, Protocol, Legal Ground, an Enemy, Army, Faith and Keys and Laws/Commandments/Statutes/Covenant,. It is made up of subjects, citizens and those who commit Treason against the Kingdom. We will learn that God is not a God of Compromise and how to Rule the Visible world from the realm of the Invisible.

So...............
WHAT IS A KINGDOM?

"A country whose head is a king or queen; a realm or region in which something or someone is dominant." The word "realm" is defined as: "Kingdom; an area or range over or within which someone or something acts, exists, or has influence." Each of us being kings in the Kingdom of God have our own domain that we are to rule in both the spirit and the natural.

The Kingdom of God is a Spiritual Kingdom.

The Kingdom is a spiritual kingdom and the King is a Spirit. We too, are expected to operate in the spiritual realm even though we have a physical body. Remember we are in this world but not of this world.

Therefore, we can know that the Kingdom of God is not of this world but of the spirit. Even though it is not of this world it is in this world and influences everything that happens on the earth. Once again putting it very simply, the Kingdom of God is God's chosen method of government or legal system. The laws by which He operates His Kingdom. The laws from which He will not waver for anyone.

It is a system by which all things are controlled and ruled by the King and His family, who are also heirs, joint heirs, co-laborers with Him in the domain called earth.

Man was created with a specific purpose on this earth; that is, dominion. The creator had a specific purpose for everything and everyone that He created.

I often tell my grandson that God created him to be boss of everything except his friends. We do not have God-given authority over another person. This authority includes things both seen and unseen.

In summary, the Kingdom of God is God's chosen legal system by which man who lives in the realm of the seen, controls everything from the unseen (spirit realm) for the purpose of "destroying the works of the devil."

Jesus told us what the Kingdom of God is and what it is like. He tried to convey to the world what the Kingdom of God is all about. So let's look at what He said.

He tells us that the Kingdom of God is like a grain of mustard seed; in other words, it appears to be the least, but when it is fully matured it is in fact the greatest among the herbs and becomes a tree, a place of rest and safety. So is the Kingdom. Right now it may not look like much but when those in the Kingdom begin to operate in their authority on the earth this Kingdom according to the Word will be the only Kingdom.

The Kingdom of God is also like leaven; when added it will affect everything with which it comes into contact. Once you begin to operate in the Kingdom of God things around you will change --NO EXCEPTIONS. They literally have no choice.

The Kingdom of God is like a treasure hidden in a field or a pearl of great price; it is so valuable that it is worth giving up everything you hold in exchange for it.

The Kingdom of God is like a great net; it catches a great catch, but the bad are rejected and thrown out and only the good are allowed to remain. In the Kingdom of God those who are citizens sow into the world the seed of the Word that produces children of the Kingdom (the righteous). Satan comes then and sows into the field of this world seeds of evil, which produce children of the kingdom of darkness (sinners). God has allowed these two to grow together on this earth until the time for the harvest or the end of time. At that point God will send forth his angel to remove the sinners (tares) and cast them into the fire where there will be weeping and wailing and gnashing of teeth. Then He will gather to himself that which is righteous.

The Government (Kingdom) of God is the most valuable knowledge that you can have. It is so valuable that it is worth giving up everything in order to be a part of it. It is knowledge that will not only change you but will change everything around you. It may appear to be small at first, but with time it will indeed take over. In the Kingdom of God only those who are in right standing with the Father are allowed to remain, and all of those who are of their father the devil will be cast out of the Kingdom.

Gates

A gate is a door-like structure that gives entrance to a location. Gates are entryways into or out of something. So are the gates in the Kingdom of God. We find gates all throughout the scriptures.

Doors

A door is a portal of entry into a building or room, consisting of a rigid plane movable on a hinge. Doors are frequently made of wood or metal. They may have a handle to help open and close, a latch to hold the door closed, and a lock that ensures the door cannot be opened without the key. In the Kingdom of God, doors, even though they are spiritual doors that cannot be seen with the natural eye, have locks and must be unlocked with keys. In most cases we are the ones who are expected to use the keys to unlock what the Kingdom holds for us, but in a few cases there are doors that have been opened for us by the King and remain open for us.

A search of the scriptures will reveal many doors to many rooms inside the Kingdom. Housed inside those rooms are things like healing, prosperity, understanding, and revelation.

Courts

The courts of this Kingdom is that area that surrounds the King or where His throne is located.

Throne

The Kingdom of God has a throne that the King sits upon. His throne is established and is eternal. It is the place where we obtain grace, mercy, justice, truth and judgment. It is also the place where we plead our case before our King who is also the just judge. It is the place where we make our petitions known before the King to receive judgments against our enemies.

Petitions based on the Word of God, which are His will and His law, will be heard in His courts and will have a judgment granted in each case. Petitions not based on the Word will not be heard in the courts of the Kingdom of God.

Before the throne of our King, it is not the number of people who approach Him but whether or not the petition is Word based that determines whether or not the petition is granted. A vast number of people flooding into his courts will not persuade Him to violate His laws. It only takes one following the rules of the Kingdom to move the world.

The King and His Kingdom

The most important part of a kingdom is the King. In this Kingdom God the Father rules as King. A king is the supreme ruler of his nation. This means that He is the highest authority. The king makes all of the laws, and the citizens have to accept them. A kingdom is not a democracy and there is no vote. The King in the Kingdom of God makes only those laws that are best for His citizens. This Kingdom is different from other kingdoms in that it is a Kingdom of Kings.

The King in this kingdom has a large family consisting of many sons and daughters. The glory of the King is the manifestation of the true nature of the King himself. His Glory is manifested in this earth by His Holy Spirit.

It is our responsibility, along with the Holy Spirit, to work to bring glory to our King, a divine display of His nature on this earth in everything that we do. The King is worthy of honor, praise and respect. We give Him honor and praise because of who He is, not because of what He does.

The worship of a king is the expression of the citizen's gratitude and appreciation to the king for his favor, privileges, and the security of being in his kingdom. Worship is also an indication of the perceived worth that the King is to the citizens. Worship always involves the offering of gifts to the king. It shows the citizen's awareness that all things he enjoys are at the pleasure of the King and the acknowledgment that it all belongs to the King. Worship also expresses one's dependency on the King. While we do not always bring physically gifts we bring Him the gift of our total commitment and love for Him.

In the Kingdom of God worship is reserved for God alone. He will not tolerate our worship of anything or anyone other than Himself.

The king's reputation is important to the King and is the source of the glory of his name. But we see in scripture the willingness of the King to make Himself of no reputation for the sake of His citizens.

Royal favor is the sovereign prerogative of the king to extend a personal law to a citizen that positions that citizen to receive special privileges and advantages that are personally protected by the King. A major part of favor in the Kingdom of God is grace and mercy. Favor is not something that I seek it is something that is placed upon me because of my relationship with the King.

Mercy is defined as forgiveness. Mercy is the fact that the king allows us the opportunity to repent when we make mistakes and sin enters our lives, and to receive forgiveness.

Grace is defined as Divine assistance in resisting sin. It is also an allowance of time granted for a debtor to correct his obligations without fear of action being taken against him. We all understand "grace period" when it comes to paying our bills. It reads something like this, "Due on the first, late after the tenth." This, of course, means that if we pay even as late as 10 days after the due date our debt will be considered paid on time.

Our King is aware of the fact that sometimes it takes time in the natural to correct things that we have allowed into our lives. He works with us to get those things corrected without bringing judgment upon us. However, there is an end to a grace period even in the Kingdom of God, but only the King himself sets that time frame.

Grace and mercy are at the discretion of the King, because only he knows the heart of the man. You might fool other men but you will never fool God. Grace is NOT an excuse to sin.

Charge

Charge is defined as an instruction or responsibility, an assignment. The King gives charges or assignments to things in the natural and to things in the spirit. Man was charged with the responsibility of overseeing the earth. I am only giving a few examples here, but as you study the Word you will find many references to assignments given by the King to both men and angels. We will identify a few more in the chapters to come

Protocol

Protocol is the rule, guideline, or document which guides how an activity should be performed. It governs the customs and regulations dealing with diplomatic formality, precedence, and etiquette. In the Kingdom of God the protocol is laid out in the scriptures for us.

There are many scriptures that dictate to us the protocol of the Kingdom. We must follow the protocol or it will not work for us.

Territory

The first act of the King in the Kingdom of God was to establish a new territory to expand his Kingdom. The territory of a kingdom is the land that is under the lordship of the King. It is his domain. The King owns his domain and can expand or extend it by the power of his might. God extended His territory to earth and established a colony here. Heaven was the primary location of the Kingdom and earth became a colony of the Kingdom

The earth belongs to the king, and that is a fact that will never change. It does not matter what it might appear to be in the natural; the Word says that is will always belong to God, and that is an eternal situation. No where will you find that any other being, neither spiritual nor physical, will ever own the territory of earth. Don't let the lies of the enemy persuade you otherwise.

Social Order of the Kingdom

In a kingdom people fall into different classifications, and based on those classifications their level of authority is determined. In the Kingdom of God, unlike other kingdoms, there are no slaves; only subjects and citizens.

A subject is:
1. A person who is under the dominion or rule of a sovereign government.
2. A person who owes allegiance to a government and lives under its protection.

These definitions given in the dictionary answer so many questions in my mind about people in the Kingdom of God and under its dominion.

Why are some saved but have no authority?

Why do some operate in great authority and others are just going to make it to heaven if they die before Jesus comes back?

This is the difference between a subject in a kingdom and a citizen within a kingdom. Citizens have rights and authority that subjects do not have. In the Kingdom of God the difference is the baptism in the Holy Spirit.

It is this power that separates subjects from citizens. Subjects are under the dominion of the Kingdom of God, but citizens have rights and authority. Unlike earthly kingdoms, in the Kingdom of God that which allows you to be a citizen is free and available to every subject in the Kingdom.

We also find references to those who are least in the kingdom and those who are great. This further shows us that there are levels that can be obtained.

It is my personal desire to obtain the highest position I can and as great a position of authority as possible in order to more effectively advance the Kingdom of God on earth and help other people.

<u>Religion</u>

Even pagan kingdoms on earth have a religion. In England we find the Church of England, and in other nations we find Islam or other paganistic religions as the recognized religion of that region or territory. The Kingdom of God on earth also has a religion or church. Unfortunately, the church we see today has no characteristics of that church.

Let's see what Jesus said about His church. Let's just look at it literally and not try to read anything into it or make it into something it is not.

Jesus asked Peter, "Who am I?" Peter responded, "You are the Son of the living God." Peter had the revelation of who Jesus was, so now we are speaking about that revelation.

Jesus said, "This revelation only came to you from the Father."

Then Jesus recognized Peter. This would seem to make no sense, because he had just addressed him by name in the preceding sentence. He was making a statement that needed to be recognized. He was saying to Peter, "You know me for who I am and I know you for who you are."

He does not recognize us until we recognize and accept Him. When something was built on a rock that rock served as the foundation for the building. Taking that into consideration, we see that the foundation upon which the church of the Kingdom is built is the revelation of who Jesus is, and that we become part of it when we accept Him. When these two revelations are in place then the gates of hell will not stand against us. The religion of the Kingdom of God is the revelation of who Jesus is: the Son of the Living God.

Priests

A priest is a person who has the authority or power to administer religious rites. We have been given two positions; one is king and the other is priest. Here we will talk about the position of priest.

The Holy Spirit gives the gifts of the Spirit to us as He wills and they are for the purpose of carrying out our duties as priests in the Kingdom. Everything that is needed to be a priest in the Kingdom of God is listed here. When you need them they are there and available as the Holy Spirit sees the need. Those gifts are Word of Wisdom, Word of Knowledge, Faith, Gifts of Healing, Working of Miracles, Prophecy, Discerning of Spirits, Divers (or different) kinds of Tongues and Interpretation of (different) Tongues. When you are FILLED with the Holy Spirit He does not just bring a few gifts He comes with all the gifts into your life BUT those gifts only operate in your life as He wills, but you have them all.

Prayer

In the Kingdom of God prayer has been very misunderstood. That is one reason we do not see answered prayer. I find five different types of prayer, and each is very simple. The way I was raised prayer always seemed like work, but at least I was taught to pray. It should also be understood that prayer is for those who are either subjects or citizens of the Kingdom, since prayer is the communication between those who serve God and the Father. So the first step to prayer is accepting Jesus as your Lord and Savior. This can only be done after the Holy Spirit has testified of Him to an individual. Accepting Jesus and confessing Him is not prayer, it is positioning ones self in the Kingdom.

The first type of prayer is the prayer of repentance, which is simply asking for forgiveness of the sin in which you have been a participant.

Second is the prayer is relationship. This is my communing with the Father and developing a deeper walk and association with Him, or you could say just getting to know Him and building a relationship. This is done in secret.

Third is the prayer of petition. This is when we express to God our needs and desires based on the Word of God. We make a lot of selfish requests without any basis in the Word for those things to be granted; that is why we do not see answers. This is praying "amiss".

Fourth is the prayer of agreement. Sometimes this is not as easy as it sounds. I have found that it is hard to find someone who will stand in faith with me in total agreement for the fulfillment of the request. Many people will say they agree, but that does not always mean they do. Two people in total agreement in the Kingdom are very dangerous against the kingdom of darkness, because nothing is impossible to them. Two in agreement do not move God they move HELL. One put 1000 (demonic spirits) to flight but two put 10,000 (demonic spirits) to flight.

Fifth is the deepest form of prayer. That is groanings that cannot be uttered. The Word says that as Jesus was on His way to the tomb of Lazarus, He groaned. This is the Spirit of God (Holy Spirit) making intercession for us to get the Will of the Father.

Then my favorite place is going beyond prayer and moving in the realm of our God-given authority on earth. Jesus commonly spent time in relationship prayer and then moved in authority or beyond prayer.

Prayer is the key to going beyond prayer.

Praying according to the Kingdom is easy and effective. It is not vain repetition nor praying amiss to consume it on our own lusts, but it is praying for the establishment and advancement of the Kingdom and the business of God's Kingdom.

In looking at the miracles of Jesus, it is interesting to note that not once did Jesus pray when He performed a miracle. The closest thing we find to prayer was when He groaned on the way to the tomb of Lazarus. We know, however, that Jesus led a life of prayer. The only recorded public prayer was when the disciples ask Him to teach them to pray. Other recorded prayers of Jesus were private. All of these miracles were done by command or authority.

Diplomatic Corps – Ambassadors

The rank of Ambassador is one of the highest within a kingdom. Ambassadors are official representatives of the kingdom and represent only the position of the government. They have no right to state their opinions or represent their opinions as those of the kingdom. They are the property of the kingdom they represent; therefore, all of their personal needs are met by their kingdom. This frees them from having to focus on their own needs so that their primary focus can be in the interest of their kingdom.

As ambassadors on earth we decree the position of our government throughout the land. These declarations are made both to those who have natural ears to hear and to the realm of the demonic forces that operate in the earth. Remember that if we are in right standing with the government we have all authority on the earth.

There is great power when an Ambassador of the Kingdom of God operating with authority decrees the Will of God on the earth.

Authority

Citizens in the Kingdom of God are given authority. This authority came when Jesus went back to the Father and He sent the Holy Spirit, who is the essence of the presence of both God the Father and God the Son on earth.

These statements were made to the disciples. They had all the knowledge of who Jesus was and what the Kingdom of God was all about, but they did not have the power or authority in the realm of the spirit to carry out what they had been assigned to do. Jesus did not send them out but told them to wait first for the power. We need to learn from this event. The only difference is that they had to "tarry" or wait for the Holy Spirit to arrive. We do not have to wait for the Holy Spirit, He is here and instantly available to anyone who sincerely wants Him to control their lives and situations. You just have to accept Him.

When the Holy Spirit arrived, they immediately went out to do the work of the Lord. Unfortunately, too many of us are still waiting for the Holy Spirit to come; we need to get the revelation, "The Holy Spirit is here." It is us that keep the manifestation from being in evidence. The assignment has been given; **now move out.**

Influence
SALT AND LIGHT

All kingdoms are committed to making the influence of the king and his will felt throughout the entire kingdom. It is time for the body of Christ (citizens of the Kingdom) to wake up. The world we live in will operate based on the influence of the kingdom that we allow to operate through us on the earth. This is done by establishing the Will of God not only in the realm of the natural eye but also in the realm of the spirit which will manifest into the natural realm.

God told us in **Genesis 1:26** that we were given dominion over the earth and everything here. Let me state again, that authority does not include people. There are only two kingdoms that influence everything; the kingdom of darkness, Satan and his demonic forces of influence, and the Kingdom of God. We MUST understand that as citizens of the Kingdom those who are in right standing with the government of God have the authority to influence all areas of this earth for Kingdom purposes.

I began years ago with small things and people thought I had lost my mind then; now the more I am moving in Kingdom influence the more people think I have totally lost it. The main statement I hear is, "Who does she think she is to think she can control things?" Understand that I do not make public the things I do in the spirit realm for the Kingdom of God; however, when I encounter a spirit from the kingdom of darkness harassing a human, I am quick to move in authority to rid that person of that spiritual influence as they are willing to release and be released from it.

It is not who I think I am; it is who I KNOW I am. I am a king in the Kingdom of God according to His word, and my authority comes from the Lord God Jehovah. Now I can believe it and act on it and change things, or I can doubt it and see things get worse. What I don't influence with the Kingdom of God I can guarantee you that Satan will influence with the kingdom of darkness.

Personally, it is my goal and intention to serve my God to the maximum and see His Kingdom come and His will be done on the earth. This is not just going to happen. This is one area where prayer has nothing to do with it except for my communication with God concerning His purposes and plans that need to be addressed on earth. He gave me and YOU the authority to carry out this assignment on earth. Satan has been very successful in gaining control because Kingdom citizens have listened to his lies and are still wasting their time asking God to do what He has already done. It is time to quit being passive and move in an aggressive mode to take back the earth that God gave us. We should be the influence that controls everything like:

Fashion - We should influence it with God's standard (modesty).
Movies/TV/Theater- We should influence it by not attending anything that has any overtone of a demonic nature (sex, violence, foul language, etc). To attend and support this is to come under the influence of a foreign government. If it is not of God, don't go – stay home, play a game, and put your money into Kingdom work.
Economy - We should be bringing the Kingdom economy into our world economy. This is one I am having a lot of fun pursuing.
Government/Politics - Elections are in our court. What are we doing (IN THE SPIRIT) to change things with Kingdom influence? (Remember this is not a flesh and blood battle). We are defeated when we view it as a natural battle.

These are just a few examples, but there are many more that can be added to the list. God is waiting for you to take the authority that He has already given you, so get up off your knees and start doing something in the spirit realm of authority.

Commonwealth

A commonwealth is the commitment of the kingdom to see that all of his citizens have equal access to the wealth and resources of the kingdom. The king is obligated to provide for his citizens and to make provision for them at his own expense for their security and their welfare. The Kingdom of God is even greater than this in seeing that every need is met.

If you truly trust in your King, you will have nothing to worry about unless you have created the problem yourself. If you create a debt, that is not His problem, it is yours. If you eat wrong and bring disease on your body, that is your problem, not His. If you go out and get into sin, creating a situation with a consequence attached, that is your problem, not His. After repentance He will assist you as you walk out of the situation, but He has never made promises to you that He would deliver you out of the things you walk yourself into. He did, however, promise to keep you IF you obey Him and follow His will.

God treats everyone in His Kingdom equally and gives each one equal opportunity to obtain different levels of position within the Kingdom.

Economic System

A good economic system guarantees each citizen access to the financial security and benefits of the kingdom. All kingdoms operate on a system that secures and sustains the strength and viability of the kingdom. The kingdom economy usually involves a taxation system, investment opportunities, and creative development programs for citizens. The Kingdom of God is the most financially secure kingdom that has ever existed because it has unlimited resources that will never cease to exist. This provides a greater security for its subjects and citizens than any investment available today.

Taxation

All kingdoms incorporate a taxation system which allows its citizens to participate in the process of maintaining the kingdom infrastructure. The system allows the citizen to share in the kingdom's commonwealth and return a set portion of the king's resources back to the king. In essence, everything in the kingdom already belongs to the king, including the taxes required from the citizen; therefore, taxation is simply the government's allowing its resources to pass through the hands of the citizen. Tithing is Kingdom taxation. The purpose of Kingdom taxation is to protect those within the Kingdom from having the devourer take what belongs to them. If you don't pay your taxes, you don't get protection; that puts it very simply.

Investment

An investment indicates that something is placed somewhere with the expectation of a return on the finance that is placed in the investment. The Word says 30/60/100 fold return. You can't get that in the world's system.

Giving

Giving to a king activates the king's obligation to demonstrate his glory and power to the giver and prove that he is a greater king than all other kings. Giving to a king in his kingdom is the acknowledgment that all things belong to that king and the citizen is grateful. Because giving to a king is impossible (since all things already belong to the king), the act of giving benefits the citizen more than the king. Thus one should never come before a king empty-handed.

**Remember you cannot out-give God,
the King of the Kingdom of God.**

Culture

This is the lifestyle of the citizens of the kingdom. It is displayed in their morals, personal values, language, dress, eating habits, etc. In the Kingdom of God we are expected to live not only good clean moral lives, but lives that are holy and acceptable before God.

There are also other things that must become part of our lifestyle, such as fasting, prayer, faith, etc. These are things that we have made events but should in fact become lifestyles.

Our Code of Ethics and our Code of Conduct can better explain our culture.

Code of Ethics

This is the standard established by the king for the behavior and social relationships of his citizens. The code of ethics is the foundation of the kingdom culture and is displayed in the lifestyle of the citizens in relationship to their morals, relationships, dress and attitude. Here we once again identify the things that we are not to do so that we can establish what we are supposed to do. We must be people of great integrity.

Do not cause your brother to fall into sin!!!!!!

Code of Conduct

This code is a set of principles that are binding on all the citizens of the kingdom and are established by the law.

Here is a list of the things that those who are citizens of God' Kingdom must live by, understanding that if you are truly in love with God and desire to please Him none of these things will be an issue. These are all things of the world, and you will love God more than you love the world. You will learn to hate everything on this list and will come to the understanding that you can do anything that you want to do, but your want to will change as you grow more in love with the King.

Maintain sexual purity reserving sexual activity only within the marriage relationship.
Stay away from everything that is unholy.
Stay away from anything that promotes **lewd and lustful thoughts and activities.**
God can be the only God in your life.
Refrain from any type of **witchcraft and manipulation.**
Love everyone - no exceptions.
Keep peace with everyone as long as it does not compromise your standing with God.
Watch all competitions that they do not become ego-feeders.

Be angry only at the things that affect the Kingdom of God, and even then do not let it cause sin in your life.
Do not let strife come between you and any man.
Obey the laws of the land.
State the Word of God only as written. Do not take it out of context or twist it.
Do not covet anything another person has.
Do not get drunk.
Do not kill.
Do not rebel against God in anything.
Do not envy another person.
Do not take anything that does not rightfully belong to you.
Only do those things **that bring glory to God** and not you.
Do not curse, use foul language or tell off color jokes.
Dress modestly in a way that is pleasing to God.
Honor your parents at all times.
Forgive everyone that offends you.
Always do the right thing regardless of what it might be.
Do not lie or even stretch the truth to the point of a lie.
Do not do anything to deceive another person.

This list is compiled directly from the word of God, so this is God's instruction, not mine. Do not deceive yourself into thinking that you can do anything you want and be part of the Kingdom of God. God will not be mocked. His standards are much higher than those of the world, and He expects His people to operate by His standards. HOW STRANGE, PECULIAR AND SEPARATED ARE YOU????

Language

Language is a method of communication. In this Kingdom there are at least three known languages.

1. Other tongues, a tongue not known to the person speaking.

2. Speaking in tongues by the spirit, also known as "praying in the spirit."

3. Then there are those times when mere words, whether by the Spirit of God or the mind of man, cannot express what we are trying to communicate. This is called "groanings". Only God Himself understands what you are expressing to Him from your spirit.

So, other than our earthly language, we see the references to other tongues, with the spirit, and a language that is referred to as groanings that cannot be uttered. These are the languages of the Kingdom of God.

Educational System

All kingdoms establish a system and program for training and educating their citizens. The Kingdom of God is no different. We have been provided a teacher to teach us all things that we need to know, and even to give us the words we need to speak when we need them.
It is not the desire of our King that we should be ignorant concerning anything; therefore, He sent us the Holy Spirit as a teacher to teach us ALL things.

He gave us the Word and the Holy Spirit as our education system. If we read the Word and listen to the teacher we will be people of great wisdom and understanding.

Administrative Services

Administration is a system through which the kingdom administers its judgments and programs to the citizens. The administrative program is designed to protect the rights and privileges of the citizens.

This really needs no explanation. These positions are gifts that were given to the body of Christ by Christ himself. He knew that the body would need order within it so that the saints could grow and be perfected for the work of the ministry. These are even today gifts and callings that are given by God. A God-called minister of the gospel is effective in bringing the saints to the point of perfection so that they can go forth and minister the gospel of the Kingdom in the earth today. This is a position that we see very little of today. We have a lot of ministers who stand and deliver a message that only helps people live a "good" life. There is no "perfecting the saints" nor teaching them their true "authority" and there is a lot of "denying the power of God" the right to operate in the midst of "His" people. There is also no real understanding nor teaching of how to do "the work of the ministry"

Not everyone who calls themselves by one of these names is placed there by God. Too many today are either self-called, people called, or mama- or daddy-called. This does an injustice not only to that man or woman, but to those over whom they have placed themselves. We need more than ever the gift of discernment to know whom God has called to lead. Seek to find those men and women, because they will bring you into a new level in the realm of the spirit.

Assignments

Assignments are tasks or jobs given to subjects and citizens by the administration. Assignments are our purpose on the earth and why we were created.

Since the only message of Jesus was the message of the Kingdom of God, this was the Kingdom message and His assignment. We find further in Mark 16 that we are also given the assignment to do as Jesus did.

The Holy Spirit has put people around you to help you fulfill your purpose. Many times, however, it is not that we do not recognize them, but we are not willing to submit to God's choice. We want to decide that for ourselves. God does not give us that option. The person who has charisma and who feeds your ego is probably not the person God has placed in your life, but the person you have chosen. If you are not constantly challenged to move forward in the Kingdom of God, you have become complacent. This is not of God.

If you have become passive in your relationship with God and His purpose for your life, you need to stop and examine where you are. As citizens of the Kingdom of God operating in the power and authority of the Holy Spirit we should be aggressively advancing the Kingdom of God in the earth, not just in our self-centered lives. If this is not where you are, get with that God-chosen person that will challenge you to be all that you can be in the Kingdom of God. It will change your life.

Constitution/Covenants/Commandments/Laws/Decrees

The Kingdom of God has a **constitution** which is a **covenant** between the King and His people.

A constitution is a covenant that expresses the mind, will, intent, desires, and purposes of the king for his citizens and kingdom. It is documented in writing and signed and sealed by the king.

Our King is a King of covenant. He not only establishes His covenant with man, He also puts it in writing for future generations. His Kingdom is from everlasting to everlasting, an eternal Kingdom.

A list of the first Ten Commandments given to Moses can be found in Exodus 20. They were mandatory. They were not optional then and they are not optional today. Even though this is a list of those first ten, a search of the scriptures will reveal others that were added as the need arose in order to keep the people of the Kingdom on the right path.

Laws

The king's word is law which cannot be changed or debated by the citizens of the land. The laws of a kingdom determine the standards that the kingdom is governed by. So it is in the Kingdom of God.

Decrees

A royal decree is a declaration of the desire of a king that becomes law to all, both in the natural realm and in the spiritual realm. You deliver a Royal decree on earth by the Holy Spirit proclaiming the Will of God on the earth.

Enemy

Everyone knows what an enemy is, and in the Kingdom of God we have an enemy who is sometimes referred to as our adversary.

> Be sober, be vigilant; because your adversary the devil, as a roaring lion, walketh about, seeking whom he may devour.
>
> 1 Peter 5:8

Let's take a minute to get to know our enemy and understand that he has a strategy for your demise. His effectiveness in your life is in your hands, not his.

He is persistent

> For the accuser of our brethren is cast down, which accused them before our God day and night.
>
> Revelation 12:10

He has a goal

> The thief cometh not, but for to steal, and to kill, and to destroy: I am come that they might have life, and that they might have it more abundantly.
> John 10:10

He has a backup plan
He shows no mercy

He has no power

And Jesus came and spake unto them, saying, All power is given unto me in heaven and in earth.

Matthew 28:18

Then he called his twelve disciples together, and gave them power and authority over all devils, and to cure diseases.

Luke 9:1

He knows the law

He watches and knows his enemy

Be sober, be vigilant; because your adversary the devil, as a roaring lion, walketh about, seeking whom he may devour:

1 Peter 5:8

He is a spirit

He is a master of deception

Put on the whole armour of God, that ye may be able to stand against the wiles of the devil.

Ephesians 6:11

He has an army that is structured

For we wrestle not against flesh and blood, but against principalities, against powers, against the rulers of the darkness of this world, against spiritual wickedness in high places.

Ephesians 6:12

He doesn't play fair

He is a liar

Ye are of your father the devil, and the lusts of your father ye will do. He was a murderer from the beginning, and abode not in the truth, because there is no truth in him. When he speaketh a lie, he speaketh of his own: for he is a liar, and the father of it.

John 8:44

He is the accuser

And I heard a loud voice saying in heaven, Now is come salvation, and strength, and the kingdom of our God, and the power of his Christ: for the accuser of our brethren is cast down, which accused them before our God day and night.

Revelation 12:10

His main weapons are lies and deception

He has a strategy

He is the master tempter

HE IS DEFEATED!!!!!

Legal Ground

Many do not realize that there are at least two aspects to the spiritual legal system. One is legal ground and the other is legal authority. Legal ground is the right of spiritual activity within a person, place or thing. Legal authority is having yourself in right standing with the government to be able to legally rule and control those things that are illegal in your territory.

Sin in a person's life gives legal ground to the enemy to operate in their lives. This is also the result of treason. When the enemy has legal ground he can go to the King and present a case against you. The King must grant his petition because you have given the right to operate in your life to the enemy.

The way to stop the legal activity of the enemy in your life is to remove any legal ground. Quit doing the things you are doing and change your choices. Then he has nothing with which to make a case against you when he comes before the King with his petitions. Then King must deny him the right to operate in your life.

Legal authority is your authority on the earth. As long as you are in right standing with the Kingdom of God and have received the power of the Holy Spirit, you are now positioned with authority over ALL DEVILS on the earth.

Army

An army secures the kingdom's territory and protects its citizens. It fights the battles on behalf of the citizens. Citizens do not fight in the army; they are protected by the army.

Charge once again is defined as an instruction or responsibility. God has given the responsibility for my protection, if I remain in right standing with the Kingdom, to the angels which are his host or army.

Here we not only see that the angels are the army of God operating in the realm of the spirit on our behalf, but they also have rank and are very organized. Since the Holy Spirit came, we receive the word of the Father by the Holy Spirit. But the angels are still actively working on our behalf, and at times deliver the Word of the Lord to us. They also actively work on behalf of the Kingdom on earth to establish the Kingdom.

Faith

My definition of faith is "a lifestyle of trusting God in every area of your life." This lifestyle becomes your shield to protect you from the attacks of the enemy. We have been taught to have faith to get things from God, but that is not what faith is all about. Yes, you have to have faith if you ever get anything from God, but here we also see faith for our protection. So I believe a valid definition of faith would be,"Trust in God in and for everything."

There is an old song that says, "Prayer is the Key to Heaven but Faith Unlocks the Door." This has become a reality to me in the last little while to a new level. The Bible says, "Without faith it is impossible to please God." It also says that if you have the "faith of a grain of mustard seed you can move mountains." And yes, here He was talking about a literal mountain made of dirt and rocks.

If you have a lock and you have the key that fits it, that to the natural eye is all you need. But the lock will never open if you don't turn the key, even if you put the key in the lock. In the Kingdom of God it is faith that activates or turns that key.

Faith has to become a natural lifestyle for those who walk in the Kingdom of God if they want to move in the power and authority of God. God told us the importance of faith in His Word.
We are told to seek first the Kingdom of God and His righteousness, and here He tells us to, above everything else, take the shield of faith. This gives us the protection that we need to stand against the enemy as we move forward in the things of the Kingdom. In the second half of this book we will look at some scriptures in the Word that show the importance of our faith to God.

Pleasing God

If you truly love God, it is your heart's desire to please Him. We find the key to pleasing God is developing a lifestyle of total trust in Him and His ways, whether you understand them or not.

Lifestyle

We MUST live every day in total dependence on Him and know that He loves us and wants nothing but the very best for us. That is, the best as He sees it, not as we see it. We must trust Him when things don't seem to be as they should or when things might not go exactly the way we think. In the end, when we look back we will see the hand of God in everything that we have walked through. We have to walk in this lifestyle with confidence, not with fear. Faith in the Kingdom is not a choice, but rather a commandment.

> And Jesus answering saith unto them, Have faith in God.
>
> Mark 11:22

What is Faith?

Faith is that which causes the things that already exist in the realm of the spirit to manifest on earth in the realm of the visible.

Everything you will ever need already exists in the heavenly realm. That is why He gave us the keys of the Kingdom to unlock on earth those things that are in the spirit realm. Your faith will either release them or cause them to remain under lock and key in the spiritual realm.

What will faith accomplish?

Your faith has no limits on what you can accomplish. We understand that with faith NOTHING is impossible. That means that anything can be accomplished through faith. **YOU ARE THE ONLY LIMIT TO WHAT IS POSSIBLE**, because with God all things are possible. There are many examples of things that are locked up because of lack of faith. It should also be noted that the things that are accomplished should be those things that are in the Will of God. Too many people take the scriptures and use them to try to manipulate situations for their own selfish personal desires. That is not what God is talking about.

Trust

We must trust God that He will take care of every need we have. God is concerned about everything that He created, and it is His desire to provide for them fully.

Levels of Faith

There are many levels of faith. Very frankly, it is up to you to determine how much your faith has grown. Every man has been given the measure of faith whether saved or lost (Romans 12:3). It is that faith within man that allows him to initially come to the saving knowledge of Jesus Christ (Ephesians 2:8).
In Matthew 8 Jesus talks about great faith of the centurion, then in Matthew 6 and 8 we see a reference to little faith. In Mark 4 He references no faith. In Matthew 17 there is a level of faith that takes sacrifice to attain, and that is with fasting and prayer. In Luke 17 the apostles ask Jesus to increase their faith and what I perceive that He said here is, "If you will just use what you have regardless of how small it is, you will increase or grow your own faith."

A mustard seed when planted will grow, but the height to which it grows is determined by the soil in which it is planted and the care it receives. I challenge you to take the faith you have, nurture it and feed it what it needs so it can grow to the level of great faith. I can think of few things greater than having God speak of me as a person of great faith.

Where is your faith?

Your faith is in your mouth. What you believe is what you speak, for out of the abundance of the heart the mouth speaks. I can know your faith level by just listening to what you speak. You need to guard your mouth until it comes into alignment with what the Word says.

The things in which you have faith are the things you are going to receive. Sometimes that is not such a good thing, because sometime people have faith in the worst. This is the way the enemy gets you. You have to see the good things of God and quit looking at the things the enemy has surrounded you with to steal your faith, because that is his plan. He does not want you to realize that you have all power and authority on the earth. He wants you to believe he does. When he gets you to this point you begin to grow your faith, but in the wrong things.

Faith brings those things you need.

You will never receive anything from God apart from faith. We see this very clearly in the Word. Wavering faith, that is, a lot of doubt mixed with trust in God, will keep you from receiving anything and everything God has to offer. You can't trust God in some things and not in others. That may work for you but it doesn't work for God. He calls you an unstable person and says that He will not give you anything. But we see that faith moves the heart of God, and when you stand in faith there is nothing that you cannot receive from God. I know that is a bold statement, but I didn't make it - God did; so do you believe Him???

Faith beyond prayer

We have been taught to connect faith and prayer, but let us look at how Jesus took faith beyond prayer and into the arena of works. In other words, He acted on the faith that He had as well as the faith that others had. James tells us that we can have faith, but if we never do anything with it we might as well not have it at all, because it is dead.

Interesting fact: Faith has life, because how can something die except first it is alive or has life? The thing that gives life to your faith is using it.

Justification

We need to first get the definition of the word justified. That is "to declare innocent or guiltless; absolve; acquit." We are not justified just because we know the Word or even because we do what the Word says and follow the law. We are only justified by the faith of Jesus. We have to work to attain the same faith that Jesus had. If it were not attainable, God would not have told us in Galatians 2:20, "and the life which I now live in the flesh I live by the faith of the Son of God, who loved me, and gave himself for me." We live in the flesh but we are to have the faith of God.

How do we get faith?

Initially every man is dealt the measure of faith; this is your seed. Faith is then fed by hearing the word of God. Practically, we have learned that whatever we hear often enough is what we begin to believe. This is why we MUST let what we hear be based on the Word of God. If we are hearing the Word but not mixing it with faith, it will profit us nothing.

So you say, "How do I fit all of this together?" Let me bring it all together for you. God has given you a measure of faith. You then use that faith to receive Jesus as your Lord and Savior, because that has to be done through faith.

Next you get into the Word of God and begin to read it, but go beyond there; read it aloud. It is important that you hear what it says with your ears, not just see what it says with your eyes.

Now it is your responsibility to begin to do what it says. The more you hear and the more you do of what it says, the more you grow. Quit arguing with God and trying to tell Him that He doesn't mean what He says. **HE MEANS EXACTLY WHAT HE SAYS,** and He does not change just because the century changed.

For instance, He told women to dress modestly. Just because fashion changed,**GOD DID NOT CHANGE OR CHANGE HIS MIND.** Just DO IT!! You will find that your faith and trust in Him will grow beyond measure. But if you waiver by making excuses you will never get anything from God.

If you "run into a bump in the road" so to speak, then the Word says,"O.K, time for fasting and prayer to build your faith to get you beyond this point" (these are my words). So just do it. Fast, pray, DO IT and move on.

The Kingdom of God is always advancing, so you must never let the enemy hang you up. Just do what needs to be done, and the more you move forward the more your faith grows. Then God will say of you, "I have not seen so great a faith," just as He said of the centurion.

More than ever receiving anything from the Kingdom, our hearts desire should be to please the Father.

Keys

Keys are the instruments by which doors are locked and unlocked. The keys of the kingdom are the principles, precepts, laws, and systems by which the kingdom functions. The keys must be learned and applied by the citizens in order to appropriate the benefits and privileges of the kingdom. These benefits and privileges are free but require a key to obtain.

The text that talks about binding and loosing are used in the context to mean lock and unlock, because that is what keys are designed to do. Here are a few keys from the scriptures

In this scripture a key is calling for the elders of the church, then the elders praying and anointing with oil. This is one key that will unlock healing and forgiveness.

Another key is to confess your faults to one another, but in these days be careful to whom you confess them. Sadly, not everyone is trust-worthy nor is everyone in right standing with the King to be able to pray that fervent prayer. However, we see that this also unlocks a door to a different type of healing.

Again we see the key to receiving is giving. In so many cases, as you search for keys in the Kingdom, you will find that they are contrary to the ways of man.

As great as knowledge is of the Kingdom of God, the next most sought after information is, "What are the Keys?" The answer to this is very easy but the process of finding them takes much more time. So I am going to try to help you at least get started discovering the Keys.

It is important that it be noted that all of these are keys **OF** the kingdom, but entrance to the Kingdom must come by discovering first the key **TO** the Kingdom.

We have been taught over and over that the scriptures are all about seed time and harvest. I believe that to be truly stated, but only to a minimal extent. The focus has been placed on this teaching in order to get people to support the work that a man or ministry has started. While the principle is good and right, the motivation is not. Not all soil is good soil and not all soil is ordained by God. You will need discernment to know where to sow.

The Word of God is a book of the law and is based on **CONDITIONAL PROMISES**. These conditional promises are all keys to unlock resources in the Kingdom of God. Some say, "What is a CONDITIONAL PROMISE?" Simply put, it is a promise that requires you to meet a condition to receive it. Seed time and harvest are a small part of this. You plant a seed, you get a harvest; you don't plant, you don't get anything. Thus the promises of God are there, but if you don't meet the condition you will not receive the promise. The KEYS OF THE KINGDOM are the conditions that you must meet to receive the promise.

Let me encourage you to search the scriptures for as many keys as you can find. The more keys you find the more resources you can unlock in the Kingdom. Just meet the condition and the promise is yours.

Treason

Treason is the ultimate form of betrayal. It is an act of aligning oneself with the enemies of their government. In the Kingdom of God treason is committed when a citizen of the Kingdom falls into alliance with the kingdom of darkness (Satan) by submitting to the influence of that kingdom (sin).

When one commits treason the first thing that happens is that they lose all of their rights and privileges as a citizen, and any authority that may have been bestowed upon them is immediately removed. It works the same in the Kingdom of God; cooperating with any spirit that is not of God is called sin and is punishable by immediately losing your authority and position in the Kingdom.

Never under estimate the strategies of the enemy, and believe me he has many. He has no power except to get you to believe a lie (wiles). Once you believe the lie and act on it, you open a door for further activity in your life by the enemy of your God. Even though he has no power, he knows you and he develops a strategy, especially designed for you, based on your strengths and weaknesses. In His Word God gives us a way to protect ourselves from the temptation of this type of attack from the enemy.

Losing your authority

Treason results in the loss of authority. One of the main questions I am asked when teaching about the Kingdom of God is, "Why don't I have that authority?" I have put together a list from the Word that God says will cause you to lose your authority. These things will keep you from walking in authority, but the real reason is that you are committing treason against the government of God by your willful cooperation with a foreign government (the kingdom of darkness, "Satan") better known as SIN.

This can happen either knowingly or unknowingly because of ignorance. This is the one thing that God said in Hosea 4:6 would destroy his people.

This is God's list, not mine. I do, however, find it very interesting that all of the things He lists have one thing in common. They are all about you: what you want, what you think you need, and how things are going to affect you.

The Kingdom of God is about Him, not you. In order to inherit His Kingdom and operate in it with full authority, you MUST take on His nature and lay aside yours. He is a holy God, and He expects those who inherit His Kingdom to be like Him.

> Because it is written, Be ye holy; for I am holy.
>
> 1 Peter 1:16

I want to make a list from the text above in order to make it easier for you to identify the things that you might have operating in your life. The first four deal with the aligning of oneself with a spirit of perversion. Once you open this door, it not only separates you from God but will lead you into even worse acts of perversion. Any type of sexual activity outside the God-ordained relationship of marriage between one man and one woman is based on your self-will and will separate you from God. This will cost you your position in the Kingdom and the loss of your authority.

Adultery- sexual relationship outside of the marriage
Fornication - sexual relationship between unmarried people
Abusers of themselves with mankind - perverted sexual acts with others
Effeminate - homosexual relationships
Uncleanness - any activity that is not "holy" before the Lord
Lasciviousness- lewd and lustful thoughts and activities
Idolatry- Placing anything or anyone before God. This can be a ball game, money, another person, etc. The thing that is your first priority is the thing that can become an idol in your heart.
Witchcraft - Any form of manipulation. This includes those times when you formulate in your mind the things you are going to say or do in order to get a desired reaction by manipulating a person or a situation.
Hatred- Should need no explanation. Extreme ungodly dislike for someone
Variance - Ungodly disagreements. Disagreeing with other and even with God about things that just don't matter
Emulations - Ungodly competition or rivalry
Wrath - Ungodly anger. If your anger is because of the way a particular thing affects you, then it is probably ungodly. Jesus got angry because of the way things affected the Kingdom of God.
Strife - Violent conflict. This can be spoken or unspoken and is an ungodly emotion.
Seditions - Taking an ungodly stand against lawful authority. (Oops, this one got me - rebellion against wearing a seat belt). Seditions are rooted in rebellion.
Heresies - Twisting the Word of God to suit your way of thinking and your situation.
Envying - A feeling of hatred and anger toward someone because of what they have or whom they are with. This also leads to covetousness,

which means wanting something or someone that belongs to another person.

Murders - Taking the God-given life of a person

Drunkenness - A state of not having full control of yourself because of an excessive amount of anything, whether it is alcohol or drugs, legal or illegal. Today it is referred to as "getting high."

Revelings - Rebellion against God and the things of God. This includes His laws, commandments and statutes, and any other directions that we have been given by His Word.

Vain glory - Glory that we seek to feed our own ego. Everything in our lives should bring glory to God, not to ourselves.

Extortioners - Obtaining something from a person by force, intimidation, or undue or illegal power.

How did you come out after this list? I pray that if you found any of these things in your life, you stopped, repented and made the decision to change your ways. Not one thing on this list is worth being out of relationship with God.

God is not a God of Compromise

Compromise is a demonic spirit. We can know this by the scripture in James.

> But above all things, my brethren, swear not, neither by heaven, neither by the earth, neither by any other oath: but let your yea be yea; and your nay, nay; lest ye fall into condemnation.

> James 5:12

We see here that the ways of God are stable and sure. They are black and white with no gray areas. Wavering is compromise.

In the eyes of God lukewarm is the same as being cold, or that is to say, being in the kingdom of darkness. The Kingdom of God and the kingdom of darkness are very defined. You are either of your Father God or of your father the devil. Do not be deceived; there is no middle ground. We can see the stand that God Himself has taken on this issue.

God's expectation of us is "holiness." Recently I read a true statement that all words have a definition, so let's look at the definition of holiness: not man's, but God's.

To be holy is to stand blameless before God.

If you stand before God thinking he will accept your excuses for the sin in your life, you need to think again. He made provision through His Son that you might walk blameless before Him. He will not accept turning your back on God. Remember, you may allow the devil to tempt you to fall into deception, but God is not fooled. Now let's go a step farther.

Darkness and light cannot be present at the same time. Either there is light or there is darkness.

God warns us that we need to know the Word and have a relationship with Him. If not, then all we can have in our lives is darkness. That is the only revelation we have of what is right or wrong.

Many people have asked me why they cannot receive the Baptism of the Holy Spirit. They have tried on so many occasions, and in many cases have given up. I can only find two reasons, so I want to talk about them.

The first is their expectation of what the in-filling of the Holy Spirit really is. Some immediately begin to speak with tongues as the Spirit gives utterance; others do not. Is one less filled than the other? The answer is no. However, the one who does not eventually will, because it is a characteristic of the nature of the Holy Spirit. The most visible sign is a change in the life of a person.

You cannot be filled with the Spirit of God and not change. Every time you enter His presence you will change a little more. The expectation of an immediate vocal manifestation does, however, cause some to think they have not received, when in fact they have. They continue to seek for the Baptism of the Holy Spirit when they should be asking for the evidence to manifest in their lives.

I also want to note here that speaking in tongues does not mean a person is filled with the Spirit of God. Remember satan has a counterfeit for everything it is your discernment that will allow you to know the real from the false.

The second reason some are not filled is that God will not place His Spirit in an unholy vessel.

Many are standing before God with all forms of sin in their lives and asking to be filled with His Spirit. Sorry, this is never going to happen. HOWEVER, and this is very important, Satan has a counterfeit for the things of God including the Holy Spirit. This has over the years given lots of people a false sense of security. That is the intent of Satan. You will not seek what you think you have.

PLUS, being able to continue in your sin and then spout out words that sound like the Holy Spirit cause many to validate the sin in their lives, thinking that God is using them, so they must be O.K. That, my friend, is exactly what Satan would have you believe. A good rule of thumb would be, "If there is SIN involved it cannot be God."

So here is my advice to each of you.

You want to receive the Holy Spirit? **Get right with God**
You want to walk in power and authority? **Get right with God**
You want to walk in righteousness? **Get right with God**
You want to live a blameless and sin free life? **Get right with God**

So how do you "Get right with God?"

Quit playing games, quit walking after and satisfying the flesh, repent and turn from the wickedness in your life. Remember, God knows your heart, so He knows if you are playing games. Just **GET REAL**.

Ruling the Visible from the Invisible

This is what the Kingdom of God is all about. Satan has been doing this throughout all of history, but we as the body of Christ have made it almost taboo. I hear too often spoken by Christians, "What will be will be," or,"God has it all under control," or, "That's just the way it is," and the list goes on and on. The truth is that some Christians are ignorant when it comes to the things of the Spirit, and it is easier to do nothing than to do something.

We have become so caught up in the distractions in our own lives that we forget that God created us for a purpose. We need to get with God's program and on His agenda, setting our own selfish agenda aside, if we are to see the coming of the King and the establishment of His Kingdom.

I was just reminded of our troops on the battlefield. When they signed on with a branch of the armed forces, they gave up their rights to allow their personal lives to supersede their service to the United States and its purposes. If the government says, "Go," they cannot say, "No, I have things I need to do." They MUST set everything aside for the purposes of the government. They leave home, family and friends for a greater purpose which they agreed to serve.

Our government is far greater and has a much greater purpose on this earth. Those who SAY they have joined with the government of God, (that is, the Kingdom of God), to see His purposes established, tend to put everything ahead of Him, and if there is any time left they will give that time to God.

In the Kingdom of God nothing can come ahead of Him. People sign on with the Kingdom of God every day. Unfortunately, they do not receive authority just by signing on. This is a deception that some have been led to believe. I want to first lay out the process so that you can understand it.

You must be "born again."

In this passage Jesus made it as plain as it can be made. First you were born into this world through your mother's womb, "born of water" and "born of flesh." Now you MUST BE "BORN OF THE SPIRIT." Being born of the "Spirit" is a two-fold process. The first is Salvation.

Salvation is made up of two parts: acceptance and righteousness.
1. Acceptance- we must accept and confess Jesus and His resurrection.

2. Righteousness or "right standing". There are things that we must do ourselves to come into a position of right standing with God the Father. One of the most important is forgiveness, that being our forgiving others, not just our being forgiven.

Well, that is plain enough. To be in right standing with the Father you must be in a state of constant forgiveness. I find it interesting that the last temptation of Christ on the cross was unforgiveness. That is why He said, "Father, forgive them: for they know not what they do."

Accepting Jesus as the Son of God and forgiving others brings us into a position in the Kingdom with the Father to receive that which He has for us. David found the secret to staying in that position of right standing as he prayed. The key to remaining in right standing is to guard your heart, your mind and your mouth.

Since you have come this far, we can talk about Kingdom authority, which is necessary if you are to rule the seen from the unseen. There is another step that MUST be taken to operate in the POWER and authority of the Kingdom of God.

It was the power of His authority that the people of that day were so amazed by. It was that power that was a witness of who He was. This power only comes through being baptized in the Holy Spirit.

In the scriptures we find that Jesus gave that same power and authority to those who were His disciples and had been BAPTIZED with the Holy Ghost (John 1:33). Many say, "That was for the disciples," and they are correct. They just don't seem to know the definition of a disciple.

A disciple is a follower and student of a mentor, teacher, or otherwise figure. We know that He was not just talking to the twelve disciples, also called apostles. As we read further we find that Jesus was not the only one who had disciples. We find mention of John's disciples and disciples of the Pharisees. In Luke we find that Jesus had many more than twelve disciples because it refers to a multitude of disciples.

It is the sole intent of a disciple to follow after the one that is disciplining him. If you do not love someone you will not follow them. We see that complete power and authority is given to disciples of Jesus (Luke 9:1, Luke 10:19, etc.

Let's stop here and sum up where we are:

I. We have accepted Jesus as the Son of God.
II. We have forgiven others and constantly continue to forgive others.
III. We have been baptized in the Holy Ghost and have received power.
IV. We have become disciples of Christ and keep His commandments.
V.   We are in right standing with the Kingdom of God based on our commitment to love God and keep His commandments.

Now we are ready to walk in authority and power of the Kingdom of God. Thus we have positioned ourselves to change the visible from the realm of the invisible. But,BEWARE, your total commitment is to always be,

"Not my will , but Thine be done."

Now to proceed forward, you need to stay in constant communion with the Father, the Son and especially your closet friend, the Holy Spirit. Learn when to pray and when to speak with authority. Begin to exercise your authority in a realm that goes beyond prayer. Let the kingdom of darkness know who you are and that you are now in control. Let's push back the kingdom of darkness and establish the throne of God here on earth.

"Let's take back what Adam gave away."

Welcome to the realm of the Spirit and the Kingdom of God.

And the rest of the story.

The rest of the book is a repeat of what you have already read with the exception that all scriptures relates to each subject are inserted for your study convenience.

As I stated at the beginning of this book this will make it easy for you to teach without having to research the scriptures. I would like, however, to receive any input from you if you like having the book written in this format.

Now let's proceed further into the Word of God to learn about His Kingdom and His Glory.

Introduction

I write this to the body of Christ under the inspiration of the Holy Spirit. It is not my opinion but is based purely on the Word of God. In the Kingdom of God there is no place for my opinion, for God only honors His Word.

The purpose of this book is to bring a revelation to the body of Christ concerning the Kingdom of which you are a part. I will endeavor to teach you how the Kingdom functions. In studying the Word, I discovered that the most important thing in the eyes of God for us is the Kingdom of God.

> But seek ye first the kingdom of God, and his righteousness; and all these things shall be added unto you.
>
> Matthew 6:33

I put things in the order of importance; therefore, if I say first, that is the thing I consider to be of greatest importance. I am created in His image and likeness, so that must also be the way God does things. This is confirmed in the fact that the only message Jesus preached was the message of the Kingdom. Further confirmed by the Scriptures is the fact that the end will not come until "the gospel of the kingdom" is preached.

> And this gospel of the kingdom shall be preached in all the world for a witness unto all nations; and then shall the end come.
>
> Matthew 24:14

If God is holding back the end of the age and the return of Jesus to the earth until the **"gospel of the Kingdom"** is preached to all nations, then it is indeed the most important message. The question is, then, "Why do we hear everything else preached except the kingdom?" I think the answer is very simple; there is a lack of revelation and a lack of understanding of the Kingdom of God.

I pray that this book will bring you closer to that revelation. My prayer is that you not only learn but begin to move in the revelation you receive. All the knowledge in the world is of no benefit to you unless you use it.

Chapter 1

Characteristics of the Kingdom

The Kingdom of God is made up of the following positions and departments. I am presenting to you the list of things that I have discovered as of this writing. There are probably more, and I will write of them as the Holy Spirit reveals them to me. The chapters to follow will address each one individually.

The Kingdom of God has:

Structure

Doors/Gates

The King

Protocol

Territory

Social Order

Religion

Prayer/Communication

Diplomatic Corps

Authority

Influence

Commonwealth

Economic System

Culture

Educational System

Language

Administrative Services

Laws/Commandments/Statutes/Covenant

Enemy

Legal Ground

Army

Faith

Keys

Treason

We will also cover

God is not a God of Compromise

Ruling the Visible from the Invisible

So................

WHAT IS A KINGDOM?

Merriam-Webster Dictionary defines "kingdom" as: "A country whose head is a king or queen; a realm or region in which something or someone is dominant."

The word "realm" is defined as: "Kingdom; an area or range over or within which someone or something acts, exists, or has influence."

The Kingdom of God has…

Structure

The Kingdom of God is a Spiritual Kingdom.

Let's verify that in the scriptures.

> Jesus answered, My kingdom is not of this world: If my kingdom were of this world, then would my servants fight, that I should not be delivered to the Jews: but now is my kingdom not from hence (this world);
>
> John 18:36

> God is a Spirit: and they that worship him must worship him in spirit and in truth.
>
> John 4:24

The Kingdom is spiritual and the King is a Spirit. We too, are expected to operate in the spiritual realm even though we have a physical body.

> For we wrestle not against flesh and blood, but against principalities, against powers, against the rulers of the darkness of this world, against spiritual wickedness in high places.
>
> Ephesians 6:12

We are in this world but not of this world.

> If ye were of the world, the world would love his own: but because ye are not of the world, but I have chosen you out of the world, therefore the world hateth you.
>
> John 15:19

Therefore, we can know that the Kingdom of God is not of this world but of the spirit. Even though it is not of this world it is in this world and influences everything that happens on the earth.

Putting it very simply, the Kingdom of God is God's chosen method of government or legal system.

> For unto us a child is born, unto us a son is given: and the government shall be upon his shoulder: and his name shall be called Wonderful, Counsellor, The mighty God, The everlasting Father, The Prince of Peace.
>
> Isaiah 9:6

It is a system by which all things are controlled and ruled by the King and His family, who are also heirs, joint heirs, co-laborers with Him in the domain of earth.

> And if children, then heirs; heirs of God, and joint-heirs with Christ; if so be that we suffer with him, that we may be also glorified together.
>
> Romans 8:17

Man was created with a specific purpose on this earth; that is, dominion. The creator had a specific purpose for everything and everyone that He created.

> 26 And God said, Let us make man in our image, after our likeness: and let them have dominion over the fish of the sea, and over the fowl of the air, and over the cattle, and over all the earth, and over every creeping thing that creepeth upon the earth.
> 27 So God created man in his own image, in the image of God created he him; male and female created he them.
>
> Genesis 1:26-27

I often tell my grandson that God created him to be boss of everything except his friends. We do not have God-given authority over another person. This authority includes things both seen and unseen.

In summary, the Kingdom of God is God's chosen legal system by which man who lives in the realm of the seen controls everything from the unseen (spirit realm) for the purpose of "destroying the works of the devil."

> He that committeth sin is of the devil; for the devil sinneth from the beginning. For this purpose the Son of God was manifested, that he might destroy the works of the devil.
>
> 1 John 3:8

We, too, are sons of God manifest in the earth.

But as many as received him, to them gave he power to become the sons of God, even to them that believe on his name:
John 1:12

For as many as are led by the Spirit of God, they are the sons of God
Romans 8:14.

Chapter 2

The Kingdom of God is like

These words were spoken often by Jesus as He tried to convey to the world what the Kingdom of God is all about. Let us therefore look at what He said.

In the following scriptures listed in both the King James and Amplified versions of the Bible you will see the description that Jesus gave of the Kingdom of God. First, I want to give you my interpretation of these scriptures.

Jesus tells us that the Kingdom of God is like a grain of mustard seed; in other words, it appears to be the least, but when it is fully matured it is in fact the greatest among the herbs and becomes a tree, a place of rest and safety.

The Kingdom of God is also like leaven; when added it will affect everything with which it comes into contact. Once you begin to operate in the Kingdom of God things around you will change --NO EXCEPTIONS.

The Kingdom of God is like a treasure hidden in a field or a pearl of great price; it is so valuable that it is worth giving up everything you hold in exchange for it.

The Kingdom of God is like a great net; it catches a great catch, but the bad are rejected and thrown out and only the good are allowed to remain.

In the Kingdom of God those who are citizens sow into the world the seed of the Word that produces children of the Kingdom (the righteous). Satan comes then and sows into the field of this world seeds of evil, which produce children of the kingdom of darkness (sinners). God has allowed these two to grow together on this earth until the time for the harvest or the end of time. At that point God will send forth his angel to remove the sinners (tares) and cast them into the fire where there will be weeping and wailing and gnashing of teeth. Then He will gather to himself that which is righteous.

The Government (Kingdom) of God is the most valuable knowledge that you can have. It is so valuable that it is worth giving up everything in order to be a part of it. It is knowledge that will not only change you but will change everything around you. It may appear to be small at first, but with time it will indeed take over. In the Kingdom of God only those who are in right standing with the Father are allowed to remain, and all of those who are of their father the devil will be cast out of the Kingdom.

King James Version
Matthew 13:24-58

> 38 The field is the world; the good seed are the children of the kingdom; but the tares are the children of the wicked one;
> 39 The enemy that sowed them is the devil; the harvest is the end of the world; and the reapers are the angels.
> 40 As therefore the tares are gathered and burned in the fire; so shall it be in the end of this world.
> 41 The Son of man shall send forth his angels, and they shall gather out of his kingdom all things that offend, and them which do iniquity;
> 42 And shall cast them into a furnace of fire: there shall be wailing and gnashing of teeth.
> 43 Then shall the righteous shine forth as the sun in the kingdom of their Father. Who hath ears to hear, let him hear.
> 44 Again, the kingdom of heaven is like unto treasure hid in a field; the which when a man hath found, he hideth, and for joy thereof goeth and selleth all that he hath, and buyeth that field.
> 45 Again, the kingdom of heaven is like unto a merchant man, seeking goodly pearls:

46 Who, when he had found one pearl of great price, went and sold all that he had, and bought it.

47 Again, the kingdom of heaven is like unto a net, that was cast into the sea, and gathered of every kind:

48 Which, when it was full, they drew to shore, and sat down, and gathered the good into vessels, but cast the bad away.

49 So shall it be at the end of the world: the angels shall come forth, and sever the wicked from among the just,

50 And shall cast them into the furnace of fire: there shall be wailing and gnashing of teeth.

51 Jesus saith unto them, Have ye understood all these things? They say unto him, Yea, Lord.

52 Then said he unto them, Therefore every scribe which is instructed unto the kingdom of heaven is like unto a man that is an householder, which bringeth forth out of his treasure things new and old.

53 And it came to pass, that when Jesus had finished these parables, he departed thence.

54 And when he was come into his own country, he taught them in their synagogue, insomuch that they were astonished, and said, Whence hath this man this wisdom, and these mighty works?

55 Is not this the carpenter's son? is not his mother called Mary? and his brethren, James, and Joses, and Simon, and Judas?

56 And his sisters, are they not all with us? Whence then hath this man all these things?

57 And they were offended in him. But Jesus said unto them, A prophet is not without honour, save in his own country, and in his own house.

58 And he did not many mighty works there because of their unbelief.

Amplified Bible

24 Another parable He set forth before them, saying, The kingdom of heaven is like a man who sowed good seed in his field.

25 But while he was sleeping, his enemy came and sowed also darnel (weeds resembling wheat) among the wheat, and went on his way.

26 So when the plants sprouted and formed grain, the darnel (weeds) appeared also.

27 And the servants of the owner came to him and said, Sir, did you not sow good seed in your field? Then how does it have darnel shoots in it?

28 He replied to them, An enemy has done this. The servants said to him, Then do you want us to go and weed them out?

29 But he said, No, lest in gathering the wild wheat (weeds resembling wheat), you root up the [true] wheat along with it.

30 Let them grow together until the harvest; and at harvest time I will say to the reapers, Gather the darnel first and bind it in bundles to be burned, but gather the wheat into my granary.

31 Another story by way of comparison He set forth before them, saying, The kingdom of heaven is like a grain of mustard seed, which a man took and sowed in his field.

32 Of all the seeds it is the smallest, but when it has grown it is the largest of the garden herbs and becomes a tree, so that the birds of the air come and find shelter in its branches.

33 He told them another parable: The kingdom of heaven is like leaven (sour dough) which a woman took and covered over in three measures of meal or flour till all of it was leavened.

34 These things all taken together Jesus said to the crowds in parables; indeed, without a parable He said nothing to them.

35 This was in fulfillment of what was spoken by the prophet: I will open My mouth in parables; I will utter things that have been hidden since the foundation of the world.

36 Then He left the throngs and went into the house. And His disciples came to Him saying, Explain to us the parable of the darnel in the field.

37 He answered, He Who sows the good seed is the Son of Man.

38 The field is the world, and the good seed means the children of the kingdom; the darnel is the children of the evil one,

39 And the enemy who sowed it is the devil. The harvest is the close and consummation of the age, and the reapers are angels.

40 Just as the darnel (weeds resembling wheat) is gathered and burned with fire, so it will be at the close of the age.

41 The Son of Man will send forth His angels, and they will gather out of His kingdom all causes of offense [persons by whom others are drawn into error or sin] and all who do iniquity and act wickedly,

42 And will cast them into the furnace of fire; there will be weeping and wailing and grinding of teeth.

43 Then will the righteous (those who are upright and in right standing with God) shine forth like the sun in the kingdom of their Father. Let him who has ears [to hear] be listening, and let him consider and perceive and understand by hearing.

44 The kingdom of heaven is like something precious buried in a field, which a man found and hid again; then in his joy he goes and sells all he has and buys that field.

45 Again the kingdom of heaven is like a man who is a dealer in search of fine and precious pearls,

46 Who, on finding a single pearl of great price, went and sold all he had and bought it.

47 Again, the kingdom of heaven is like a dragnet which was cast into the sea and gathered in fish of every sort.

48 When it was full, men dragged it up on the beach, and sat down and sorted out the good fish into baskets, but the worthless ones hey threw away.

49 So it will be at the close and consummation of the age. The angels will go forth and separate the wicked from the righteous (those who are upright and in right standing with God)

50 And cast them [the wicked] into the furnace of fire; there will be weeping and wailing and grinding of teeth.

51 Have you understood all these things [parables] taken together? They said to Him, Yes, Lord.

52 He said to them, Therefore every teacher and interpreter of the Sacred Writings who has been instructed about and trained for the kingdom of heaven and has become a disciple is like a householder who brings forth out of his storehouse treasure that is new and [treasure that is] old [the fresh as well as the familiar].

53 When Jesus had finished these parables (these comparisons), He left there.

54 And coming to His own country [Nazareth], He taught in their synagogue so that they were amazed with bewildered wonder, and said, Where did this Man get this wisdom and these miraculous powers?

55 Is not this the carpenter's Son? Is not His mother called Mary? And are not His brothers James and Joseph and Simon and Judas?

56 And do not all His sisters live here among us? Where then did this Man get all this?

57 And they took offense at Him [they were repelled and hindered from acknowledging His authority, and caused to stumble]. But Jesus said to them, A prophet is not without honor except in his own country and in his own house.

58 And He did not do many works of power there, because of their unbelief (their lack of faith in the divine mission of Jesus).

Chapter 3

Gates

A gate is a door-like structure that gives entrance to a location. Gates are entryways into or out of something. So are the gates in the Kingdom of God.

> Enter into his gates with thanksgiving, and into his courts with praise: be thankful unto him, and bless his name.
> Psalm 100:4

> And I say also unto thee, That thou art Peter, and upon this rock I will build my church; and the gates of hell shall not prevail against it.
> Matthew 16:18

Not only are there gates that surround the courts of heaven, but there are also gates that are positioned at the entryway into hell. The scripture here tells us that they will not be able to keep us out. They cannot stand against the citizens of the Kingdom of God.

Doors

A door is a portal of entry into a building or room, consisting of a rigid plane movable on a hinge. Doors are frequently made of wood or metal. They may have a handle to help open and close, a latch to hold the door closed, and a lock that ensures the door cannot be opened without the key. In the Kingdom of God, doors, even though they are spiritual doors that cannot be seen with the natural eye, have locks and must be unlocked with keys. In most cases we are the ones who are expected to use the keys to unlock what the Kingdom holds for us, but in a few cases there are doors that have been opened for us by the King and remain open for us.

> Verily, verily, I say unto you, He that entereth not by the door into the sheepfold, but climbeth up some other way, the same is a thief and a robber.
> John 10:1

> But he that entereth in by the door is the shepherd of the sheep.
> John 10:2

> Then said Jesus unto them again, Verily, verily, I say unto you, I am the door of the sheep.
> John 10:7

> I am the door: by me if any man enter in, he shall be and shall go in and out, and find pasture.
> John 10:9

A search of the scriptures will reveal many doors to many rooms inside the Kingdom. Housed inside those rooms are things like healing, prosperity, understanding, and revelation.

Courts

These are scriptures that show the existence of the courts of heaven.

> Enter into his gates with thanksgiving, and into his courts with praise: be thankful unto him, and bless his name.
>
> Psalm 100:4

14 And this is the confidence that we have in him, that, if we ask any thing according to his will, he heareth us:
15 And if we know that he hear us, whatsoever we ask, we know that we have the petitions that we desired of him.

1 John 5:14-15

Throne

The Kingdom of God has a throne that the King sits upon.

> And thine house and thy kingdom shall be established for ever before thee: thy throne shall be established forever.
>
> 2 Samuel 7:16
>
> Thy throne, O God, is for ever and ever: the sceptre of thy kingdom is a right sceptre.
> Psalm 45:6
>
> Justice and judgment are the habitation of thy throne: mercy and truth shall go before thy face.
>
> Psalm 89:14
>
> Let us therefore come boldly unto the throne of grace, that we may obtain mercy, and find grace to help in time of need.
> Hebrews 4:16

His throne is established and is eternal. It is the place where we obtain grace, mercy, justice, truth and judgment. It is also the place where we plead our case before our King who is also the just judge. It is the place where we make our petitions known before the King to receive judgments against our enemies.

> 14 And this is the confidence that we have in him, that, if we ask any thing according to his will, he heareth us:

15 And if we know that he hear us, whatsoever we ask, we know that we have the petitions that we desired of him.

1 John 5:14-15

Petitions based on the Word of God, which are His will and His law, will be heard in His courts and will have a judgment granted in each case. Petitions not based on the Word will not be heard in the courts of the Kingdom of God.

Chapter 4

The King and His Kingdom

The most important part of a kingdom is the King. In this Kingdom God the Father rules as King. A king is the supreme ruler of his nation. This means that He is the highest authority. The king makes all of the laws, and the citizens have to accept them. A kingdom is not a democracy and there is no vote. The King in the Kingdom of God makes only those laws that are best for His citizens. This Kingdom is different from other kingdoms in that it is a Kingdom of Kings.

> These shall make war with the Lamb, and the Lamb shall overcome them: for he is Lord of lords, and King of kings: and they that are with him are called, and chosen, and faithful.
>
> Revelation 17:14

The king in this kingdom has a large family consisting of many sons and daughters.

> 4 But when the fullness of the time was come, God sent forth his Son, made of a woman, made under the law,
> 5 To them that were under the law, that we might receive the adoption of sons.
> 6 And because ye are sons, God hath sent forth the Spirit of his Son into your hearts, crying, Abba, Father.
> 7 Wherefore thou art no more a servant, but a son; and if a son, then an heir of God through Christ.
>
> Galatians 4:4-7

The glory of the king is the manifestation of the true nature of the king himself.

> The heavens declare the glory of God; the skies proclaim the work of His hands.
>
> Psalm 19:1 – (NIV)

It is our responsibility, along with the Holy Spirit, to work to bring glory to our King, a divine display of His nature on this earth in everything that we do. The King is worthy of honor, praise and respect. We give Him honor and praise because of who He is, not because of what He does.

> Saying with a loud voice, Worthy is the Lamb that was slain to receive power, and riches, and wisdom, and strength, and honour, and glory, and blessing.
>
> Revelation 5:12

The worship of a king is the expression of the citizen's gratitude and appreciation to the king for his favor, privileges, and the security of being in his kingdom. Worship is also an indication of the perceived worth that the king is to the citizen. Worship always involves the offering of gifts to the king. It shows the citizen's awareness that all things he enjoys are at the pleasure of the king and the acknowledgment that it all belongs to the king. Worship also expresses one's dependency on the king.

> For thou shalt worship no other god: for the LORD, whose name is Jealous, is a jealous God:
>
> Exodus 34:14

In the Kingdom of God worship is reserved for God alone. He will not tolerate our worship of anything or anyone other than Himself.

The king's reputation is important to the king and is the source of the glory of his name. But we see the willingness of the King to make Himself of no reputation for our sakes.

> For the sake of His great name the LORD will not reject His people, because the LORD was pleased to make you His own.
>
> 1 Samuel 12:22 – (NIV)

> But made himself of no reputation, and took upon him the form of a servant, and was made in the likeness of men:
>
> Philippians 2:7

Royal favor is the sovereign prerogative of the king to extend a personal law to a citizen that positions that citizen to receive special privileges and advantages that are personally protected by the king. A major part of favor in the Kingdom of God is grace and mercy.

Mercy is defined as forgiveness. Mercy is the fact that the king allows us the opportunity to repent when we make mistakes and sin enters our lives, and to receive forgiveness.

Grace is defined as Divine assistance in resisting sin. It is also an allowance of time granted for a debtor to correct his obligations without fear of action being taken against him. We all understand "grace period" when it comes to paying our bills. It reads something like this, "Due on the first, late after the tenth." This, of course, means that if we pay even as late as 10 days after the due date our debt will be considered paid on time.

Our King is aware of the fact that sometimes it takes time in the natural to correct things that we have allowed into our lives. He works with us to get those things corrected without bringing judgment upon us. However, there is an end to a grace period even in the Kingdom of God, but only the King himself sets that time frame.

> And he said, I will make all my goodness pass before thee, and I will proclaim the name of the LORD before thee; and will be gracious to whom I will be gracious, and will shew mercy on whom I will shew mercy.
>
> Exodus 33:19

Grace and mercy are at the discretion of the King, because only he knows the heart of the man. You might fool other men but you will never fool God.

Charge is defined as an instruction or responsibility, an assignment. The King gives charges or assignments to things in the natural and to things in the spirit. Man was charged with the responsibility of overseeing the earth.

> 28 And God blessed them, and God said unto them, Be fruitful, and multiply, and replenish the earth, and subdue it: and have dominion over the fish of the sea, and over the fowl of the air, and over every living thing that moveth upon the earth.
>
> Genesis 1:28

> And he said unto them, Go ye into all the world, and preach the gospel to every creature.
>
> Mark 16:15

The angels are also given charges or assignments.

> 11 For he shall give his angels charge over thee, to keep thee in all thy ways.
> 12 They shall bear thee up in their hands, lest thou dash thy foot against a stone.
>
> Psalm 91:11-12

I am only giving a few examples here, but as you study the Word you will find many references to assignments given by the King to both men and angels. We will identify a few more in the chapters to come

Protocol

Protocol is the rule, guideline, or document which guides how an activity should be performed. It governs the customs and regulations dealing with diplomatic formality, precedence, and etiquette. In the Kingdom of God the protocol is laid out in the scriptures for us.

> Let us therefore come boldly unto the throne of grace, that we may obtain mercy, and find grace to help in time of need.
>
> Hebrews 4:16

> Enter into his gates with thanksgiving, and into his courts with praise: be thankful unto him, and bless his name.
>
> Psalm 100:4

Follow peace with all men, and holiness, without which no man shall see the Lord:

Hebrews 12:14

Jesus answered, Verily, verily, I say unto thee, Except a man be born of water and of the Spirit, he cannot enter into the kingdom of God.

John 3:5

Jesus saith unto him, I am the way, the truth, and the life: no man cometh unto the Father, but by me.

John 14:6

And said, Verily I say unto you, Except ye be converted, and become as little children, ye shall not enter into the kingdom of heaven.

Matthew 18:3

Whosoever therefore shall humble himself as this little child, the same is greatest in the kingdom of heaven.

Matthew 18:4

And Jesus said unto him, No man, having put his hand to the plough, and looking back, is fit for the kingdom of God.

Luke 9:62

There are many other scriptures that dictate to us the protocol of the Kingdom. We must follow the protocol or it will not work for us.

Chapter 5

Territory

The first act of the King in the Kingdom of God was to establish a new territory to expand his kingdom. The territory of a kingdom is the land that is under the lordship of the king. It is his domain. The king owns his domain and can expand or extend it by the power of his might. God extended His territory to earth and established a colony here.

> In the beginning God created the heaven and the earth. Heaven was the primary location of the Kingdom and earth became a colony of the Kingdom.
>
> Genesis 1:1

> 34 And at the end of the days I Nebuchadnezzar lifted up mine eyes unto heaven, and mine understanding returned unto me, and I blessed the most High, and I praised and honoured him that liveth for ever, whose dominion is an everlasting dominion, and his kingdom is from generation to generation:
> 35 And all the inhabitants of the earth are reputed as nothing: and he doeth according to his will in the army of heaven, and among the inhabitants of the earth: and none can stay his hand, or say unto him, What doest thou?
>
> Daniel 4:34-35

> For the earth is the Lord's, and the fullness thereof.
>
> 1 Corinthians 10:26

The earth belongs to the king, and that is a fact that will never change. It does not matter what it might appear to be in the natural; the Word says that is will always belong to God, and that is an eternal situation. Nowhere will you find that any other being, neither spiritual nor physical, will ever own the territory of earth.

Chapter 6

Social Order of the Kingdom

In a kingdom people fall into different classifications, and based on those classifications their level of authority is determined. In the Kingdom of God, unlike other kingdoms, there are no slaves; only subjects and citizens.

A subject is:

1. A person who is under the dominion or rule of a sovereign government.

2. A person who owes allegiance to a government and lives under its protection.

These definitions given in the dictionary answer so many questions in my mind about people in the Kingdom of God and under its dominion.

Why are some saved but have no authority?

Why do some operate in great authority and others are just going to make it to heaven if they die before Jesus comes back?

This is the difference between a subject in a kingdom and a citizen within a kingdom. Citizens have rights and authority that subjects do not have. In the Kingdom of God the difference is the baptism in the Holy Spirit.

> But ye shall receive power, after that the Holy Ghost is come upon you: and ye shall be witnesses unto me both in Jerusalem, and in all Judaea, and in Samaria, and unto the uttermost part of the earth.
>
> Acts 1:8

It is this power that separates subjects from citizens. Subjects are under the dominion of the Kingdom of God, but citizens have rights and authority. Unlike earthly kingdoms, in the Kingdom of God that which allows you to be a citizen is free and available to every subject in the Kingdom.

> Fear not, little flock; for it is your Father's good pleasure to give you the kingdom.
> Luke 12:32

> 20 But we are citizens of the state (commonwealth, homeland) which is in heaven, and from it also we earnestly and patiently await [the coming of] the Lord Jesus Christ (the Messiah) [as] Savior,
>
> Philippians 3:20 (Amplified Bible)

> But ye are a chosen generation, a royal priesthood, an holy nation, a peculiar people; that ye should shew forth the praises of him who hath called you out of darkness into his marvellous light;
> 1 Peter 2:9

We also find references to those who are least in the kingdom and those who are great. This further shows us that there are levels that can be obtained.

> Verily I say unto you, Among them that are born of women there hath not risen a greater than John the Baptist: notwithstanding he that is least in the kingdom of heaven is greater than he.
> Matthew 11:11

> Whosoever therefore shall humble himself as this little child, the same is greatest in the kingdom of heaven.
>
> Matthew 18:4

It is my personal desire to obtain the highest position I can and as great a position of authority as possible in order to more effectively advance the Kingdom of God on earth and help other people.

<u>Religion</u>

Even pagan kingdoms on earth have a religion. In England we find the Church of England, and in other nations we find Islam or other paganistic religions as the recognized religion of that region or territory. The Kingdom of God on earth also has a religion or church. Unfortunately, the church we see today has no characteristics of that church.

> 15 He saith unto them, But whom say ye that I am?
> 16 And Simon Peter answered and said, Thou art the Christ, the Son of the living God.
> 17 And Jesus answered and said unto him, Blessed art thou, Simon Barjona: for flesh and blood hath not revealed it unto thee, but my Father which is in heaven.
> 18 And I say also unto thee, That thou art Peter, and upon this rock I will build my church; and the gates of hell shall not prevail against it.
> Matthew 16:15-18

What was Jesus saying here? Let's just look at it literally and not try to read anything into it or make it into something it is not.

Jesus asked Peter, "Who am I?" Peter responded, "You are the Son of the living God." Peter had the revelation of who Jesus was, so now we are speaking about that revelation.

Jesus said, "This revelation only came to you from the Father." Then Jesus recognized Peter. This would seem to make no sense, because he had just addressed him by name in the preceding sentence. He was making a statement that needed to be recognized. He was saying to Peter, "You know me for who I am and I know you for who you are." He does not recognize us until we recognize and accept Him. When something was built on a rock, the rock served as the foundation for the building. Taking that into consideration, we see that the foundation upon which the church of the Kingdom is built is the revelation of who Jesus is, and that we become part of it when we accept Him. When these two revelations are in place then the gates of hell will not stand against us. The religion of the Kingdom of God is the revelation of who Jesus is: the Son of the Living God.

Priests

A priest is a person who has the authority or power to administer religious rites. We have been given two positions; one is king and the other is priest. Here we will talk about the position of priest.

> And hast made us unto our God kings and priests: and we shall reign on the earth.
>
> Revelation 5:10

The Holy Spirit gives the gifts of the Spirit to us as He wills and they are for the purpose of carrying out our duties as priests in the Kingdom.

> 4 Now there are diversities of gifts, but the same Spirit.
> 5 And there are differences of administrations, but the same Lord.
> 6 And there are diversities of operations, but it is the same God which worketh all in all.
> 7 But the manifestation of the Spirit is given to every man to profit withal.
> 8 For to one is given by the Spirit the word of wisdom; to another the word of knowledge by the same Spirit;
> 9 To another faith by the same Spirit; to another the gifts of healing by the same Spirit;
> 10 To another the working of miracles; to another prophecy; to another discerning of spirits; to another divers kinds of tongues; to another the interpretation of tongues:
> 11 But all these worketh that one and the selfsame Spirit, dividing to every man severally as he will.
>
> 1 Corinthians 12:4-11

Everything that is needed to be a priest in the Kingdom of God is listed here. When you need them they are there and available as the Holy Spirit sees the need.

Prayer

In the Kingdom of God prayer has been very misunderstood. That is one reason we do not see answered prayer. I find five different types of prayer, and each is very simple. The way I was raised prayer always seemed like work, but at least I was taught to pray. It should also be understood that prayer is for those who are either subjects or citizens of the Kingdom, since prayer is the communication between those who serve God and the Father. So the first step to prayer is accepting Jesus as your Lord and Savior. This can only be done after the Holy Spirit has testified of Him to an individual. Accepting Jesus and confessing Him is not prayer.

The first type of prayer is the prayer of repentance, which is simply asking for forgiveness of the sin in which we have been a participant.

> If we confess our sins, he is faithful and just to forgive us our sins, and to cleanse us from all unrighteousness.
>
> 1 John 1:9

Second is the prayer is relationship. This is my communing with the Father and developing a deeper walk and association with Him, or you could say just getting to know Him. This is done in secret.

> But thou, when thou prayest, enter into thy closet, and when thou hast shut thy door, pray to thy Father which is in secret; and thy Father which seeth in secret shall reward thee openly.
>
> Matthew 6:6

Third is the prayer of petition. This is when we express to God our needs and desires based on the Word of God. We make a lot of selfish requests without any basis in the Word for those things to be granted; that is why we do not see answers.

> 14 And this is the confidence that we have in him, that, if we ask anything according to his will, he heareth us:

> 15 And if we know that he hear us, whatsoever we ask, we know that we have the petitions that we desired of him.
>
> 1 John 5:14-15

Fourth is the prayer of agreement. Sometimes this is not as easy as it sounds. I have found that it is hard to find someone who will stand in faith with you in total agreement for the fulfillment of the request. Many people will say they agree, but that does not always mean they do.

> Again I say unto you, That if two of you shall agree on earth as touching any thing that they shall ask, it shall be done for them of my Father which is in heaven.
>
> Matthew 18:19

Two people in total agreement in the Kingdom are very dangerous against the kingdom of darkness, because nothing is impossible to them.

Fifth is the deepest form of prayer. That is groanings that cannot be uttered. The Word says that as Jesus was on His way to the tomb of Lazarus, He groaned. This is the Spirit of God making intercession for us to get the Will of the Father.

> Likewise the Spirit also helpeth our infirmities: for we know not what we should pray for as we ought: but the Spirit itself maketh intercession for us with groanings which cannot be uttered.
>
> Romans 8:26

> When Jesus therefore saw her weeping, and the Jews also weeping which came with her, he groaned in the spirit, and was troubled.
>
> John 11:33

Then my favorite place is going beyond prayer and moving in the realm of our God-given authority on earth. Jesus commonly spent time in relationship prayer and then moved in authority or beyond prayer.

Prayer is the key to going beyond prayer.

> For he said unto him, Come out of the man, thou unclean spirit.
>
> Mark 17:8

> And Jesus rebuked the devil; and he departed out of him: and the child was cured from that very hour.
>
> Luke 17:18

Praying according to the Kingdom is easy and effective. It is not vain repetition nor praying amiss to consume it on our own lusts, but it is praying for the establishment and advancement of the Kingdom and the business of God's Kingdom.

> Ye ask, and receive not, because ye ask amiss, that ye may consume it upon your lusts.
>
> James 4:3

> But seek ye first the kingdom of God, and his righteousness; and all these things shall be added unto you.
>
> Matthew 6:33

Let's look at the miracles of Jesus. It is interesting to note that not once did Jesus pray when He performed a miracle. The closest thing we find to prayer was when He groaned on the way to the tomb of Lazarus. We know, however, that Jesus led a life of prayer. The only recorded public prayer was when the disciples ask Him to teach them to pray. Other recorded prayers of Jesus were private. All of these miracles were done by command or authority.

Turning the Water into Wine

> 7 Jesus saith unto them, Fill the water pots with water. And they filled them up to the brim.
> 8 And he saith unto them, Draw out now, and bear unto the governor of the feast. And they bare it.
>
> John 2:7-8

Healing of the Nobleman's Son

50 Jesus saith unto him, Go thy way; thy son liveth. And the man believed the word that Jesus had spoken unto him, and he went his way.
51 And as he was now going down, his servants met him, and told him, saying, Thy son liveth.

John 4:50-51

Deliverance of the Demoniac in the Synagogue

And Jesus rebuked him, saying, Hold thy peace, and come out of him.

Mark 1:25

Healing of Peter's Mother-in-law

And he came and took her by the hand, and lifted her up; and immediately the fever left her, and she ministered unto them.

Mark 1:31

The First Draught of Fishes

Now when he had left speaking, he said unto Simon, Launch out into the deep, and let down your nets for a draught.

Luke 5:4

Cleansing the Leper

And Jesus, moved with compassion, put forth his hand, and touched him, and saith unto him, I will; be thou clean.

Mark 1:41

Healing the Paralytic

5 When Jesus saw their faith, he said unto the sick of the palsy, Son, thy sins be forgiven thee.
11 I say unto thee, Arise, and take up thy bed, and go thy way into thine house.

Mark 2:5&11

Healing of the Man at Bethesda

Jesus saith unto him, Rise, take up thy bed, and walk.

John 5:8

Healing the Man with the Withered Hand

And looking round about upon them all, he said unto the man, Stretch forth thy hand. And he did so: and his hand was restored whole as the other.

Luke 6:10

Healing of the Centurion's Servant

Wherefore neither thought I myself worthy to come unto thee: but say in a word, and my servant shall be healed.

Luke 7:17

Raising of the Widow's Son from Nain

And he came and touched the bier: and they that bare him stood still. And he said, Young man, I say unto thee, Arise.

Luke 7:14

Casting out of the Dumb and Blind Spirit

And he was casting out a devil, and it was dumb. And it came to pass, when the devil was gone out, the dumb spake; and the people wondered.

Luke 11:14

Stilling the Storm

And he arose, and rebuked the wind, and said unto the sea, Peace, be still. And the wind ceased, and there was a great calm.

Mark 4:39

Healing the Demoniac at Gadara

For he said unto him, Come out of the man, thou unclean spirit.

Mark 5:8

Healing the Woman with the Issue of Blood

And he said unto her, Daughter, thy faith hath made thee whole; go in peace, and be whole of thy plague.

Mark 5: 34

The Raising of Jairus' Daughter

And he took the damsel by the hand, and said unto her, Talitha cumi; which is, being interpreted, Damsel, I say unto thee, arise.

Mark 5:41

Healing of the Two Blind Men

Then touched he their eyes, saying, According to your faith be it unto you.

Matthew 9:29

Casting out the "Speech Impaired" Spirit

And when the devil was cast out, the dumb spake:

Matthew 9:33

Feeding of the 5,000

And Jesus took the loaves; and when he had given thanks, he distributed to the disciples,

John 6:11

Walking on the Water

25 And in the fourth watch of the night Jesus went unto them, walking on the sea.
29 And he said, Come.

Matthew 14:25&29

Delivering the Syrophoenician's Daughter

Then Jesus answered and said unto her, O woman, great is thy faith: be it unto thee even as thou wilt. And her daughter was made whole from that very hour.

Matthew15: 28

Healing the Deaf and Dumb Man

And looking up to heaven, he sighed, and saith unto him, Ephphatha, that is, Be opened.

Mark 7:34

Feeding the 4,000

And he commanded the people to sit down on the ground: and he took the seven loaves, and gave thanks, and brake, and gave to his disciples to set before them; and they did set them before the people.

Mark 8:6

Healing the Blind Man of Bethsaida

And he took the blind man by the hand, and led him out of the town; and when he had spit on his eyes, and put his hands upon him, he asked him if he saw ought.

Mark 8:23

Casting the Demon out of the Lunatic Boy

When Jesus saw that the people came running together, he rebuked the foul spirit, saying unto him, Thou dumb and deaf spirit, I charge thee, come out of him, and enter no more into him.

Mark 9:25

The Coin in the Fish's Mouth

Notwithstanding, lest we should offend them, go thou to the sea, and cast an hook, and take up the fish that first cometh up; and when thou hast opened his mouth, thou shalt find a piece of money: that take, and give unto them for me and thee.

Matthew 17:27

Healing of the Man Born Blind

6 When he had thus spoken, he spat on the ground, and made clay of the spittle, and he anointed the eyes of the blind man with the clay,
7 And said unto him, Go, wash in the pool of Siloam, (which is by interpretation, Sent.) He went his way therefore, and washed, and came seeing.

John 9:6-7

Healing of the Woman with the 18-Year Infirmity

And when Jesus saw her, he called her to him, and said unto her, Woman, thou art loosed from thine infirmity.

Luke 13:12

Healing the Man with Dropsy

And they held their peace. And he took him, and healed him, and let him go;

Luke 14:4

The Raising of Lazarus

23 Jesus saith unto her, Thy brother shall rise again.
43 And when he thus had spoken, he cried with a loud voice, Lazarus, come forth.

John 11:23&43

Cleansing of the Ten Lepers

13 And they lifted up their voices, and said, Jesus, Master, have mercy on us.
14 And when he saw them, he said unto them, Go shew yourselves unto the priests. And it came to pass, that, as they went, they were cleansed.

Luke 17:13-14

Healing of Blind Bartimeaus

And Jesus said unto him, Go thy way; thy faith hath made thee whole. And immediately he received his sight, and followed Jesus in the way.

Mark 10: 52

Cursing of the Fig Tree

And Jesus answered and said unto it, No man eat fruit of thee hereafter forever. And his disciples heard it.

Mark 11:14

Healing of Malchus' Ear

And Jesus answered and said, Suffer ye thus far. And he touched his ear, and healed him.

Luke 22: 51

Second Draught of Fishes

And he said unto them, Cast the net on the right side of the ship, and ye shall find. They cast therefore, and now they were not able to draw it for the multitude of fishes.

John 21:6

These should be our examples of how we are to operate in the earth today. When He left He said greater things than this shall you do. We will never do them until we move as He did in a realm beyond prayer.

Chapter 7

Diplomatic Corps – Ambassadors

The rank of Ambassador is one of the highest within a kingdom. Ambassadors are official representatives of the kingdom and represent only the position of the government. They have no right to state their opinions or represent their opinions as those of the kingdom. They are the property of the kingdom they represent; therefore, all of their personal needs are met by their kingdom. This frees them from having to focus on their own needs so that their primary focus can be in the interest of their kingdom.

> 21 Then said Jesus to them again, Peace be unto you: as my Father hath sent me, even so send I you.
> 22 And when he had said this, he breathed on them, and saith unto them, Receive ye the Holy Ghost:
> 23 Whosoever sins ye remit, they are remitted unto them; and whose soever sins ye retain, they are retained.
>
> John 20:21-23

> Now then we are ambassadors for Christ, as though God did beseech you by us: we pray you in Christ's stead, be ye reconciled to God.
>
> 2 Corinthians 5:20

> For which I am an ambassador in bonds: that therein I may speak boldly, as I ought to speak.
>
> Ephesians 6:20

As ambassadors on earth we decree the position of our government through- out the land. These declarations are made both to those who have natural ears to hear and to the realm of the demonic forces that operate in the earth.

Remember that if we are in right standing with the government we have all authority on the earth.

> Thou shalt also decree a thing, and it shall be established unto thee: and the light shall shine upon thy ways.
>
> Job 22:28

There is great power when an Ambassador of the Kingdom of God operating with authority decrees the Will of God on the earth.

Authority

Citizens in the Kingdom of God are given authority. This authority came when Jesus went back to the Father and He sent the Holy Spirit, who is the essence of the presence of both God the Father and God the Son on earth.

> 16 And I will pray the Father, and he shall give you another Comforter, that he may abide with you for ever;
> 17 Even the Spirit of truth; whom the world cannot receive, because it seeth him not, neither knoweth him: but ye know him; for he dwelleth with you, and shall be in you.
>
> John 14:16-17

> But ye shall receive power, after that the Holy Ghost is come upon you: and ye shall be witnesses unto me both in Jerusalem, and in all Judaea, and in Samaria, and unto the uttermost part of the earth.
>
> Acts 1:8

> And, behold, I send the promise of my Father upon you: but tarry ye in the city of Jerusalem, until ye be endued with power from on high.
>
> Luke 24:49

These statements were made to the disciples. They had all the knowledge of who Jesus was and what the Kingdom of God was all about, but they did not have the power or authority in the realm of the spirit to carry out what they had been assigned to do. Jesus did not send them out but told them to wait first for the power. We need to learn from this event. The only difference is that they had to "tarry" or wait for the Holy Spirit to arrive. We do not have to wait, for the Holy Spirit is here and instantly available to anyone who sincerely wants Him to control their lives and situations. When the Holy Spirit arrived, they immediately went out to do the work of the Lord. Unfortunately too many of us are still waiting for the Holy Spirit to come; we need to get the revelation, "The Holy Spirit is here." It is us that keep the manifestation from being in evidence. The assignment has been given;

now move out.

> Then he called his twelve disciples together, and gave them power and authority over all devils, and to cure diseases.
>
> Luke 9:1

Chapter 8

Influence

SALT AND LIGHT

All kingdoms are committed to making the influence of the king and his will felt throughout the entire kingdom.

> 19 Go ye therefore, and teach all nations, baptizing them in the name of the Father, and of the Son, and of the Holy Ghost:
> 20 Teaching them to observe all things whatsoever I have commanded you: and, lo, I am with you always, even unto the end of the world. Amen.
> Matthew 28:19-20

Things of this world have temporary existence but the things of the kingdom of God are eternal

> While we look not at the things which are seen, but at the things which are not seen: for the things which are seen are temporal; but the things which are not seen are eternal.
> 2 Corinthians 4:18

It is time for the body of Christ (citizens of the Kingdom) to wake up. The world we live in will operate based on the influence of the kingdom that we allow to operate through us on the earth. This is done by establishing the Will of God not only in the realm of the natural eye but also in the realm of the spirit which will manifest into the natural realm. God told us in Genesis 1:26 that we were given dominion over the earth and everything here. Let me state again, that authority does not include people. There are only two kingdoms that influence everything; the kingdom of darkness, Satan and his demonic forces of influence, and the Kingdom of God. We MUST understand that as citizens of the Kingdom those who are in right standing with the government of God have the authority to influence all areas of this earth for Kingdom purposes.

I began years ago with small things and people thought I had lost my mind then; now the more I am moving in Kingdom influence the more people think I have totally lost it. The main statement I hear is, "Who does she think she is to think she can control things?" Understand that I do not make public the things I do in the spirit realm for the Kingdom of God; however, when I encounter a spirit from the kingdom of darkness harassing a human, I am quick to move in authority to rid that person of that spiritual influence as they are willing to release and be released from it.

It is not who I think I am; it is who I KNOW I am. I am a king in the Kingdom of God according to His word, and my authority comes from the Lord God Jehovah. Now I can believe it and act on it and change things, or

I can doubt it and see things get worse. What I don't influence with the Kingdom of God I can guarantee you that Satan will influence with the kingdom of darkness.

Personally, it is my goal and intention to serve my God to the maximum and see His Kingdom come and His will be done. This is not just going to happen. This is one area where prayer has nothing to do with it except for my communication with God concerning His purposes and plans that need to be addressed on earth. He gave me and YOU the authority to carry out this assignment on earth. Satan has been very successful in gaining control because Kingdom citizens have listened to his lies and are still wasting their time asking God to do what He has already done. It is time to quit being passive and move in an aggressive mode to take back the earth that God gave us. We should be the influence that controls everything like*:*

Fashion - We should influence it with God's standard (modesty) .

Movies/TV/Theater- We should influence it by not attending anything that has any overtone of a demonic nature (sex, violence, foul language, etc). To attend and support this is to come under the influence of a foreign government. If it is not of God, don't go – stay home, play a game, and put your money into Kingdom work.

Economy - We should be bringing the Kingdom economy into our world economy. This is one I am having a lot of fun pursuing.

Government/Politics - Elections are in our court. What are we doing (IN THE SPIRIT) to change things with Kingdom influence? (Remember this is not a flesh and blood battle).

These are just a few examples, but there are many more that can be added to the list. God is waiting for you to take the authority that He has already given you, so get up off your knees and start doing something in the spirit realm of authority.

Chapter 9

Commonwealth

A commonwealth is the commitment of the kingdom to see that all of his citizens have equal access to the wealth and resources of the kingdom. The king is obligated to provide for his citizens and to make provision for them at his own expense for their security and their welfare. The Kingdom of God is even greater than this in seeing that every need is met.

> 31 Therefore take no thought, saying, What shall we eat? or, What shall
> we drink? or, Wherewithal shall we be clothed?
> 32 (For after all these things do the Gentiles seek:) for your heavenly Father knoweth that ye have need of all these things.
> 33 But seek ye first the kingdom of God, and his righteousness; and all these things shall be added unto you.
> 34 Take therefore no thought for the morrow: for the morrow shall take thought for the things of itself. Sufficient unto the day is the evil thereof.
>
> Matthew 6:31-34

If you truly trust in your King, you will have nothing to worry about unless you have created the problem yourself. If you create a debt, that is not His problem, it is yours. If you eat wrong and bring disease on your body, that is your problem, not His. If you go out and get into sin, creating a situation with a consequence attached, that is your problem, not His. After repentance He will assist you as you walk out of the situation, but He has never made promises to you that He would deliver you out of the things you walk yourself into. He did, however, promise to keep you IF you obey Him and follow His will. God treats everyone in His Kingdom equally and gives each one equal opportunity to obtain different levels of position within the Kingdom.

> Then Peter opened his mouth, and said, Of a truth I perceive that God is no respecter of persons:
>
> Acts 10:34

Chapter 10

Kingdom Economic System

A good economic system guarantees each citizen access to the financial security and benefits of the kingdom. All kingdoms operate on a system that secures and sustains the strength and viability of the kingdom. The kingdom economy usually involves a taxation system, investment opportunities, and creative development programs for citizens. The Kingdom of God is the most financially secure kingdom that has ever existed because it has unlimited resources that will never cease to exist. This provides a greater security for its subjects and citizens than any investment available today.

> For the earth is the Lord's, and the fullness thereof.
>
> 1 Corinthians 10:26

Taxation

All kingdoms incorporate a taxation system which allows its citizens to participate in the process of maintaining the kingdom infrastructure. The system allows the citizen to share in the kingdom's commonwealth and return a set portion of the king's resources back to the king. In essence, everything in the kingdom already belongs to the king, including the taxes required from the citizen; therefore, taxation is simply the government's allowing its resources to pass through the hands of the citizen. Tithing is Kingdom taxation. The purpose of Kingdom taxation is to protect those within the Kingdom from having the devourer take what belongs to them. If you don't pay your taxes , you don't get protection; that puts it very simply.

> 8 Will a man rob God? Yet ye have robbed me. But ye say, Wherein have we robbed thee? In tithes and offerings.
> 9 Ye are cursed with a curse: for ye have robbed me, even this whole nation.
> 10 Bring ye all the tithes into the storehouse, that there may be meat in mine house, and prove me now herewith, saith the LORD of hosts, if I will not open you the windows of heaven, and pour you out a blessing, that there shall not be room enough to receive it.
> 11 And I will rebuke the devourer for your sakes, and he shall not destroy the fruits of your ground; neither shall your vine cast her fruit before the time in the field, saith the LORD of hosts.
> 12 And all nations shall call you blessed: for ye shall be a delightsome land, saith the LORD of hosts.
>
> Malachi 3:8-12

<u>Investments</u>

An investment indicates that something is placed somewhere with the expectation of a return on the finance that is placed in the investment.

> Give, and it shall be given unto you; good measure, pressed down, and shaken together, and running over, shall men give into your bosom. For with the same measure that ye mete withal it shall be measured to you again.
>
> Luke 6:38

> But lay up for yourselves treasures in heaven, where neither moth nor rust doth corrupt, and where thieves do not break through nor steal:
>
> Matthew 6:20

<u>Giving</u>

Giving to a king activates the king's obligation to demonstrate his glory and power to the giver and prove that he is a greater king than all other kings. Giving to a king in his kingdom is the acknowledgment that all things belong to that king and the citizen is grateful. Because giving to a king is impossible (since all things already belong to the king), the act of giving benefits the citizen more than the king. Thus one should never come before a king empty-handed.

> 6 But this I say, He which soweth sparingly shall reap also sparingly; and he which soweth bountifully shall reap also bountifully.
> 7 Every man according as he purposeth in his heart, so let him give; not grudgingly, or of necessity: for God loveth a cheerful giver.
>
> 2 Corinthians 9:6-7

Remember you cannot out-give God,

the King of the Kingdom of God.

Chapter 11

Kingdom Culture

This is the lifestyle of the citizens of the kingdom. It is displayed in their morals, personal values, language, dress, eating habits, etc.

> 15 I do not ask that You will take them out of the world, but that You will keep and protect them from the evil one.
> 16 They are not of the world (worldly, belonging to the world), [just] as I am not of the world.
> 17 Sanctify them [purify, consecrate, separate them for Yourself, make them holy] by the Truth; Your Word is Truth.
> 18 Just as You sent Me into the world, I also have sent them into the world.
> 19 And so for their sake and on their behalf I sanctify (dedicate, consecrate) Myself, that they also may be sanctified (dedicated, consecrated, made holy) in the Truth.
>
> John 17:15-19 (Amplified Bible)

In the Kingdom of God we are expected to live not only good clean moral lives, but lives that are holy and acceptable before God. There are also other things that must become part of our lifestyle, such as fasting, prayer, faith, etc. These are things that we have made events but should in fact become lifestyles.

Our Code of Ethics and our Code of Conduct can better explain our culture.

Code of Ethics

This is the standard established by the king for the behavior and social relationships of his citizens. The code of ethics is the foundation of the kingdom culture and is displayed in the lifestyle of the citizens in relationship to their morals, relationships, dress and attitude. Here we once again identify the things that we are not to do so that we can establish what we are supposed to do. We must be people of great integrity.

> 9 Do you not know that the unrighteous and the wrongdoers will not inherit or have any share in the kingdom of God? Do not be deceived (misled): neither the impure and immoral, nor idolaters, nor adulterers, nor those who participate in homosexuality,
> 10 Nor cheats (swindlers and thieves), nor greedy graspers, nor drunkards, nor foulmouthed revilers and slanderers, nor extortioners and robbers will inherit or have any share in the kingdom of God.
> 11 And such some of you were [once]. But you were washed clean (purified by a complete atonement for sin and made free from the guilt of sin), and you were consecrated (set apart, hallowed), and you were justified [pronounced righteous, by trusting] in the name of the Lord Jesus Christ and in the [Holy] Spirit of our God.
>
> 1 Corinthians 6:9-11 (Amplified Bible)

> In like manner also, that women adorn themselves in modest apparel,
> 1Timothy 2:9

> Let the words of my mouth, and the meditation of my heart, be acceptable in thy sight, O LORD, my strength, and my redeemer.
> Psalm 19:14

> Be ye not unequally yoked together with unbelievers: for what fellowship hath righteousness with unrighteousness? and what communion hath light with darkness?
>
> 2 Corinthians 6:14

Do not cause your brother to fall into sin!!!!!!

Code of Conduct

This code is a set of principles that are binding on all the citizens of the kingdom and are established by the law.

> Honour thy father and thy mother: and, Thou shalt love thy neighbour as thyself.
> Matthew 19:19

> 4 Charity suffereth long, and is kind; charity envieth not; charity vaunteth not itself, is not puffed up,
> 5 Doth not behave itself unseemly, seeketh not her own, is not easily provoked, thinketh no evil;
> 6 Rejoiceth not in iniquity, but rejoiceth in the truth;
> 7 Beareth all things, believeth all things, hopeth all things, endureth all things.
> 1 Corinthians 13:4-7

> 22 But the fruit of the Spirit is love, joy, peace, longsuffering, gentleness, goodness, faith,
> 23 Meekness, temperance: against such there is no law.
>
> Galatians 5: 22-23

> By this shall all men know that ye are my disciples, if ye have love one to another.
> John 13:35

Here is a list of the things that those who are citizens must live by, understanding that if you are truly in love with God and desire to please Him none of these things will be an issue. These are all things of the world, and you will love God more than you love the world. You will learn to hate everything on this list and will come to the understanding that you can do anything that you want to do, but your want to will change as you grow more in love with the King.

> Love not the world, neither the things that are in the world. If any man love the world, the love of the Father is not in him.
>
> 1 John 2:15

Maintain sexual purity reserving sexual activity only within the marriage relationship.

Stay away from everything that is unholy.

Stay away from anything that promotes lewd and lustful thoughts and activities.

God can be the only God in your life.

Refrain from any type of witchcraft and manipulation.

Love everyone - no exceptions.

Keep peace with everyone as long as it does not compromise your standing with God.

Watch all competitions that they do not become ego-feeders.

Be angry only at the things that affect the Kingdom of God, and even then do not let it cause sin in your life.

Do not let strife come between you and any man.

Obey the laws of the land.

State the Word of God only as written. Do not take it out of context or twist it.

Do not covet anything another person has.

Do not get drunk.

Do not kill.

Do not rebel against God in anything.

Do not envy another person.

Do not take anything that does not rightfully belong to you.

Only do those things that bring glory to God and not you.

Do not curse, use foul language or tell off color jokes.

Dress modestly in a way that is pleasing to God.

Honor your parents at all times.

Forgive everyone that offends you.

Always do the right thing regardless of what it might be.

Do not lie or even stretch the truth to the point of a lie.

Do not do anything to deceive another person.

> Wherefore come out from among them, and be ye separate, saith the Lord, and touch not the unclean thing; and I will receive you.
> 2 Corinthians 6:17

> But ye are a chosen generation, a royal priesthood, an holy nation, a peculiar people; that ye should shew forth the praises of him who hath called you out of darkness into his marvelous light;
> 1 Peter 2:9

This list is compiled directly from the word of God, so this is God's instruction, not mine. Do not deceive yourself into thinking that you can do anything you want and be part of the Kingdom of God. God will not be mocked. His standards are much higher than those of the world, and He expects His people to operate by His standards.

HOW STRANGE, PECULIAR AND SEPARATED ARE YOU????

Language

Language is a method of communication. In this Kingdom there are at least three known languages.

> And they were all filled with the Holy Ghost, and began to speak with other tongues, as the Spirit gave them utterance.
> Acts 2: 4

Speaking in tongues is also known as "praying in the spirit." We see in the next scripture reference made to this.

> What is it then? I will pray with the spirit, and I will pray with the understanding also: I will sing with the spirit, and I will sing with the understanding also.
>
> 1 Corinthians 14:15

Then there are those times when mere words, whether by the Spirit of God or the mind of man, cannot express what we are trying to communicate.

> Likewise the Spirit also helpeth our infirmities: for we know not what we should pray for as we ought: but the Spirit itself maketh intercession for us with groanings which cannot be uttered.
>
> Romans 8:26

So, other than our earthly language, we see the references to other tongues, with the spirit, and a language that is referred to as groanings that cannot be uttered.

Educational System

All kingdoms establish a system and program for training and educating their citizens. The Kingdom of God is no different. We have been provided a teacher to teach us all things that we need to know, and even to give us the words we need to speak when we need them.

> But the Comforter, which is the Holy Ghost, whom the Father will send in my name, he shall teach you all things, and bring all things to your remembrance, whatsoever I have said unto you.
>
> John 14:26

It is not the desire of our King that we should be ignorant concerning anything; therefore, He sent us the Holy Spirit as a teacher to teach us ALL things.

> For I would not, brethren, that ye should be ignorant of this mystery, lest ye should be wise in your own conceits; that blindness in part is happened to Israel, until the fullness of the Gentiles be come in.
>
> Romans 11:25
>
> Moreover, brethren, I would not that ye should be ignorant, how that all our fathers were under the cloud, and all passed through the sea;
>
> 1 Corinthians 10:1
>
> Now concerning spiritual gifts, brethren, I would not have you ignorant.
>
> 1 Corinthians 12:1

He gave us the Word and the Holy Spirit as our education system. If we read the Word and listen to the teacher we will be people of great wisdom and understanding.

Chapter 12

Administrative Services

Administration is a system through which the kingdom administers its judgments and programs to the citizens. The administrative program is designed to protect the rights and privileges of the citizens.

> 11 And he gave some, apostles; and some, prophets; and some, evangelists; and some, pastors and teachers;
> 12 For the perfecting of the saints, for the work of the ministry, for the edifying of the body of Christ:
>
> Ephesians 4:11-12

This really needs no explanation. These positions are gifts that were given to the body of Christ by Christ himself. He knew that the body would need order within it so that the saints could grow and be perfected for the work of the ministry. These are even today gifts and callings that are given by God. A God-called minister of the gospel is effective in bringing the saints to the point of perfection so that they can go forth and minister the gospel of the Kingdom in the earth today.

Not everyone who calls themselves by one of these names is placed there by God. Too many today are either self-called, people called, or mama- or daddy-called. This does an injustice not only to that man or woman, but to those over whom they have placed themselves. We need more than ever the gift of discernment to know whom God has called to lead. Seek to find those men and women, because they will bring you into a new level in the realm of the spirit.

> 13 But he answered and said, Every plant, which my heavenly Father hath not planted, shall be rooted up.
> 14 Let them alone: they be blind leaders of the blind. And if the blind lead the blind, both shall fall into the ditch.

Matthew 15: 13-14

Assignments are tasks or jobs given to subjects and citizens by the administration. Assignments are our purpose on the earth and why we were created.

> 18 "The Spirit of the LORD is upon Me, Because He has anointed Me to preach the gospel to the poor; He has sent Me to heal the brokenhearted, to proclaim liberty to the captives and recovery of sight to the blind, to set at liberty those who are oppressed;
> 19 To proclaim the acceptable year of the LORD."

Luke 4:18-19

Since the only message of Jesus was the message of the Kingdom of God, this was the Kingdom message and His assignment. We find further in Mark 16 that we are also given the assignment to do as Jesus did.

> And he said unto them, Go ye into all the world, and preach the gospel to every creature.

Mark 16:15

The Holy Spirit has put people around you to help you fulfill your purpose. Many times, however, it is not that we do not recognize them, but we are not willing to submit to God's choice. We want to decide that for ourselves. God does not give us that option. The person who has charisma and who feeds your ego is probably not the person God has placed in your life, but the person you have chosen. If you are not constantly challenged to move forward in the Kingdom of God, you have become complacent. This is not of God.

If you have become passive in your relationship with God and His purpose for your life, you need to stop and examine where you are. As citizens of the Kingdom of God operating in the power and authority of the Holy Spirit we should be aggressively advancing the Kingdom of God in the earth, not just in our self-centered lives constantly. If this is not where you are, get with that God-chosen person that will challenge you to be all that you can be in the Kingdom of God. It will change your life.

Chapter 13

Constitution/Covenants/Commandments/Laws/Decrees

The Kingdom of God has a constitution which is a covenant between the King and His people. A constitution is a covenant that expresses the mind, will, intent, desires, and purposes of the king for his citizens and kingdom. It is documented in writing and signed and sealed by the king.

> And I, behold, I establish my covenant with you, and with your seed after you;
>
> Genesis 9:9

> Because that Abraham obeyed my voice, and kept my charge, my commandments, my statutes, and my laws.
>
> Genesis 26:5

> And I will establish my covenant with you, neither shall all flesh be cut off any more by the waters of a flood; neither shall there any more be a flood to destroy the earth.
>
> Genesis 9:11

> In the same day the LORD made a covenant with Abram, saying, Unto thy seed have I given this land, from the river of Egypt unto the great river, the river Euphrates:
>
> Genesis 15:18

> And I will establish my covenant between me and thee and thy seed after thee in their generations for an everlasting covenant, to be a God unto thee, and to thy seed after thee.
>
> Genesis 17:7

Our King is a King of covenant. He not only establishes His covenant with man, He also puts it in writing for future generations. His Kingdom is from everlasting to everlasting, an eternal kingdom.

Commandments

> It is good for me that I have been afflicted; that I might learn thy statutes.
>
> Psalm 119:71

Commandments are directives that MUST be obeyed. They are mandatory.

> Thy hands have made me and fashioned me: give me understanding, that I may learn thy commandments.
>
> Psalm 119:73

Here is a list of the first Ten Commandments given to Moses. They were mandatory. They were not optional then and they are not optional today.

> 3 Thou shalt have no other gods before me.
> 4 Thou shalt not make unto thee any graven image, or any likeness of any thing that is in heaven above, or that is in the earth beneath, or that is in the water under the earth.
> 5 Thou shalt not bow down thyself to them, nor serve them: for I the LORD thy God am a jealous God, visiting the iniquity of the fathers upon the children unto the third and fourth generation of them that hate me;
> 6 And shewing mercy unto thousands of them that love me, and keep my commandments.
> 7 Thou shalt not take the name of the LORD thy God in vain; for the LORD will not hold him guiltless that taketh his name in vain.
> 8 Remember the sabbath day, to keep it holy.

9 Six days shalt thou labour, and do all thy work:
10 But the seventh day is the sabbath of the LORD thy God: in it thou shalt not do any work, thou, nor thy son, nor thy daughter, thy manservant, nor thy maidservant, nor thy cattle, nor thy stranger that is within thy gates:
11 For in six days the LORD made heaven and earth, the sea, and all that in them is, and rested the seventh day: wherefore the LORD blessed the sabbath day, and hallowed it.
12 Honour thy father and thy mother: that thy days may be long upon the land which the LORD thy God giveth thee.
13 Thou shalt not kill.
14 Thou shalt not commit adultery.
15 Thou shalt not steal.
16 Thous halt not bear false witness against thy neighbour.
17 Thou shalt not covet thy neighbour's house, thou shalt not covet thy neighbour's wife, nor his manservant, nor his maidservant, nor his ox, nor his ass, nor any thing that is thy neighbour's.

Exodus 20:3-17

Even though this is a list of those first ten, a search of the scriptures will reveal others that were added as the need arose in order to keep the people of the Kingdom on the right path.

Laws

The king's word is law which cannot be changed or debated by the citizens of the land. The laws of a kingdom determine the standards that the kingdom is governed by.

> For as many as are of the works of the law are under the curse: for it is written, Cursed is every one that continueth not in all things which are written in the book of the law to do them.
>
> Galatians 3:10

> 71 It is good for me that I have been afflicted; that I might learn thy statutes.

> 72 The law of thy mouth is better unto me than thousands of gold and silver.
> 73 Thy hands have made me and fashioned me: give me understanding, that I may learn thy commandments.
>
> Psalm 119:71-73

Decrees

A royal decree is a declaration of the desire of a king that becomes law to all, both in the natural realm and in the spiritual realm.

> Thou shalt also decree a thing, and it shall be established unto thee: and the light shall shine upon thy ways.
>
> Job 22:28

Here is a biblical example of a decree that was made by an earthly king.

> Therefore I make a decree, That every people, nation, and language, which speak any thing amiss against the God of Shadrach, Meshach, and Abednego, shall be cut in pieces, and their houses shall be made a dunghill: because there is no other God that can deliver after this sort.
>
> Daniel 3:29

Here is a decree made by our King.

> I tell you the truth, until heaven and earth disappear, not the smallest letter, not the least stroke of a pen, will by any means disappear from the Law until everything is accomplished.
>
> Matthew 5:18 (NIV)

Chapter 14

Enemy

Everyone knows what an enemy is, and in the Kingdom of God we have an enemy who is sometimes referred to as our adversary.

> Be sober, be vigilant; because your adversary the devil, as a roaring lion, walketh about, seeking whom he may devour.
>
> 1 Peter 5:8

Let's take a minute to get to know our enemy and understand that he has a strategy for your demise. His effectiveness in your life is in your hands, not his.

He is persistent

> For the accuser of our brethren is cast down, which accused them before our God day and night.
>
> Revelation 12:10

He has a goal

> The thief cometh not, but for to steal, and to kill, and to destroy: I am come that they might have life, and that they might have it more abundantly.
>
> John 10:10

He has a backup plan

He shows no mercy

He has no power

> And Jesus came and spake unto them, saying, All power is given unto me in heaven and in earth.
>
> Matthew 28:18

> Then he called his twelve disciples together, and gave them power and authority over all devils, and to cure diseases.
>
> Luke 9:1

He knows the law

He watches and knows his enemy

> Be sober, be vigilant; because your adversary the devil, as a roaring lion, walketh about, seeking whom he may devour.
>
> 1 Peter 5:8

He is a spirit

He is a master of deception

> Put on the whole armour of God, that ye may be able to stand against the wiles of the devil.
>
> Ephesians 6:11

He has an army that is structured

> For we wrestle not against flesh and blood, but against principalities, against powers, against the rulers of the darkness of this world, against spiritual wickedness in high places.
>
> Ephesians 6:12

He doesn't play fair

He is a liar

> Ye are of your father the devil, and the lusts of your father ye will do. He was a murderer from the beginning, and abode not in the truth, because there is no truth in him.

When he speaketh a lie, he speaketh of his own: for he is a liar, and the father of it.

John 8:44

He is the accuser

And I heard a loud voice saying in heaven, Now is come salvation, and strength, and the kingdom of our God, and the power of his Christ: for the accuser of our brethren is cast down, which accused them before our God day and night.

Revelation 12:10

His main weapons are lies and deception

He has a strategy

He is the master tempter

HE IS DEFEATED!!!!!

For whatsoever is born of God overcometh the world: and this is the victory that overcometh the world, even our faith.

1 John 5:4

And Jesus came and spake unto them, saying, All power is given unto me in heaven and in earth.

Matthew 28:18

Behold, I give unto you power to tread on serpents and scorpions, and over all the power of the enemy: and nothing shall by any means hurt you.

Luke 10:19

Chapter 15

Legal Ground

Many do not realize that there are at least two aspects to the spiritual legal system. One is legal ground and the other is legal authority. Legal ground is the right of spiritual activity within people, place or things. Legal authority is having yourself in right standing with the government to be able to legally rule and control those things that are illegal in your territory.

Sin in a person's life gives legal ground to the enemy to operate in their lives. This is also the result of treason. When the enemy has legal ground he can go to the King and present a case against you. The King must grant his petition because you have given that right to the enemy. The way to stop the legal activity of the enemy in your life is to remove any legal ground. Then he has nothing with which to make a case when he comes before the King with his petitions. The King must deny him the right to operate in your life.

Legal authority is your authority on the earth. As long as you are in right standing with the Kingdom of God and have received the power of the Holy Spirit, you are now positioned with authority over ALL DEVILS on the earth. Refer to Chapter 7 on Authority.

Chapter 16

Army

An army secures the kingdom's territory and protects its citizens. It fights the battles on behalf of the citizens. Citizens do not fight in the army; they are protected by the army.

> And all the inhabitants of the earth are reputed as nothing: and he doeth according to his will in the army of heaven, and among the inhabitants of the earth: and none can stay his hand, or say unto him, What doest thou?
>
> Daniel 4:35

> 9 Because thou hast made the LORD, which is my refuge, even the most High, thy habitation;
> 10 There shall no evil befall thee, neither shall any plague come nigh thy dwelling.
> 11 For he shall give his angels charge over thee, to keep thee in all thy ways.
> 12 They shall bear thee up in their hands, lest thou dash thy foot against a stone.
>
> Psalm 91:9-12

Charge is defined as an instruction or responsibility. God has given the responsibility for my protection, if I remain in right standing with the Kingdom, to the angels which are his host or army.

> A thousand shall fall at thy side, and ten thousand at thy right hand; but it shall not come nigh thee.
>
> Psalm 91:7

> For thy Maker is thine husband; the LORD of hosts is his name; and thy Redeemer the Holy One of Israel; The God of the whole earth shall he be called.
>
> Isaiah 54:5

> 13 And it came to pass, when Joshua was by Jericho, that he lifted up his eyes and looked, and, behold, there stood a man over against him with his sword drawn in his hand: and Joshua went unto him, and said unto him, Art thou for us, or for our adversaries?
> 14 And he said, Nay; but as captain of the host of the LORD am I now come. And Joshua fell on his face to the earth, and did worship, and said unto him, What saith my Lord unto his servant?
> 15 And the captain of the LORD's host said unto Joshua, Loose thy shoe from off thy foot; for the place whereon thou standest is holy. And Joshua did so.
>
> Joshua 5:13-15

Here we not only see that the angels are the army of God operating in the realm of the spirit on our behalf, but they also have rank and are very organized. Since the Holy Spirit came, we receive the word of the Father by the Holy Spirit. But the angels are still actively working on our behalf, and at times deliver the Word of the Lord to us. They also actively work on behalf of the Kingdom on earth to establish the Kingdom.

Chapter 17

Faith

My definition of faith is "a lifestyle of trusting God in every area of your life." This lifestyle becomes your shield to protect you from the attacks of the enemy. We have been taught to have faith to get things from God, but that is not what faith is all about. Yes, you have to have faith if you ever get anything from God, but here we also see faith for our protection. So I believe a valid definition of faith would be,"Trust in God in and for everything."

There is an old song that says, "Prayer is the Key to Heaven but Faith Unlocks the Door." This has become a reality to me in the last little while to a new level. The Bible says, "Without faith it is impossible to please God." It also says that if you have the "faith of a grain of mustard seed you can move mountains."

> And Jesus said unto them, Because of your unbelief: for verily I say unto you, If ye have faith as a grain of mustard seed, ye shall say unto this mountain, Remove hence to yonder place; and it shall remove; and nothing shall be impossible unto you.
>
> Matthew 17:20

And yes, here He was talking about a literal mountain made of dirt and rocks.

If you have a lock and you have the key that fits it, that to the natural eye is all you need. But the lock will never open if you don't turn the key, even if you put the key in the lock. In the Kingdom of God it is faith that activates or turns that key.

Faith has to become a natural lifestyle for those who walk in the Kingdom of God if they want to move in the power and authority of God. God told us the importance of faith in His Word.

> Above all, taking the shield of faith, wherewith ye shall be able to quench all the fiery darts of the wicked.
>
> Ephesians 6:16

We are told to seek first the Kingdom of God and His righteousness, and here He tells us to, above everything else, take the shield of faith. This gives us the protection that we need to stand against the enemy as we move forward in the things of the Kingdom. Let's look at some scriptures in the Word that show the importance of our faith to God.

Pleasing God

If you truly love God, it is your heart's desire to please Him. Here we find the key to pleasing God. Once again it is developing a lifestyle of total trust in Him and His ways, whether you understand them or not.

> But without faith it is impossible to please him: for he that cometh to God must believe that he is, and that he is a rewarder of them that diligently seek him.
>
> Hebrews 11:6

Lifestyle

This is a further example of a lifestyle of faith. We MUST live every day in total dependence on Him and know that He loves us and wants nothing but the very best for us. That is, the best as He sees it, not as we see it. We must trust in Him when things don't seem to be as they should or when things might not go exactly the way we think. In the end, when we look back we will see the hand of God in everything that we have walked through. We have to walk in this lifestyle with confidence, not with fear.

> Behold, his soul which is lifted up is not upright in him: but the just shall live by his faith.
>
> Habakkuk 2:4

> 6 Therefore we are always confident, knowing that, whilst we are at home in the body, we are absent from the Lord:
> 7 (For we walk by faith, not by sight:)
> 8 We are confident, I say, and willing rather to be absent from the body, and to be present with the Lord.
> 9 Wherefore we labour, that, whether present or absent, we may be accepted of him.
> 10 For we must all appear before the judgment seat of Christ; that every one may receive the things done in his body, according to that he hath done, whether it be good or bad.
>
> 2 Corinthians 5:6-10

Faith in the Kingdom is not a choice, but rather a commandment.

> And Jesus answering saith unto them, Have faith in God.
>
> Mark 11:22

What is Faith?

Faith is that which causes the things that already exist in the realm of the spirit to manifest on earth in the realm of the visible.

Everything you will ever need already exists in the heavenly realm. That is why He gave us the keys of the Kingdom to unlock on earth those things that are in the spirit realm. Your faith will either release them or cause them to remain under lock and key in the spiritual realm.

> Now faith is the substance of things hoped for, the evidence of things not seen.
>
> Hebrews 11:1

> Through faith we understand that the worlds were framed by the word of God, so that things, which are seen, were not made of things which do appear.
>
> Hebrews 11:3

What will faith accomplish?

Your faith has no limits on what you can accomplish. We see here that with faith NOTHING is impossible. That means that anything can be accomplished through faith. YOU ARE THE ONLY LIMIT TO WHAT IS POSSIBLE, because with God all things are possible. Let's look at an example of things that are locked up because of lack of faith. It should also be noted that the things that are accomplished should be those things that are in the will of God. Too many people take these scriptures and use them to try to manipulate situations for their own selfish personal desires. That is not what God is talking about.

> 19 Then came the disciples to Jesus apart, and said, Why could not we cast him out?
> 20 And Jesus said unto them, Because of your unbelief: for verily I say unto you, If ye have faith as a grain of mustard seed, ye shall say unto this mountain, Remove hence to yonder place; and it shall remove; and nothing shall be impossible unto you.
>
> Matthew 17:19-20

> Jesus answered and said unto them, Verily I say unto you, If ye have faith, and doubt not, ye shall not only do this which is done to the fig tree, but also if ye shall say unto this mountain, Be thou removed, and be thou cast into the sea; it shall be done.
>
> Matthew 21:21

Trust

We must trust God that He will take care of every need we have. Here we see that He is concerned about everything that He created, and it is His desire to provide for them fully.

> Wherefore, if God so clothe the grass of the field, which today is, and tomorrow is cast into the oven, shall he not much more clothe you, O ye of little faith?
>
> Matthew 6:30

Levels of Faith

There are many levels of faith. Very frankly, it is up to you to determine how much your faith has grown. Every man has been given the measure of faith whether saved or lost (Romans 12:3). It is that faith within man that allows him to initially come to the saving knowledge of Jesus Christ (Ephesians 2:8).

In Matthew 8 Jesus talks about great faith of the centurion, then in Matthew 6 and 8 we see a reference to little faith. In Mark 4 He references no faith. In Matthew 17 there is a level of faith that takes sacrifice to attain, and that is with fasting and prayer. In Luke 17 the apostles ask Jesus to increase their faith and what I perceive that He said here is, "If you will just use what you have regardless of how small it is, you will increase or grow your own faith."A mustard seed when planted will grow, but the height to which it grows is determined by the soil in which it is planted and the care it receives.

I challenge you to take the faith you have, nurture it and feed it what it needs so it can grow to the level of great faith. I can think of few things greater than having God speak of me as a person of great faith.

> For by grace are ye saved through faith; and that not of yourselves: it is the gift of God:
>
> Ephesians 2:8

For I say, through the grace given unto me, to every man that is among you, not to think of himself more highly than he ought to think; but to think soberly, according as God hath dealt to every man the measure of faith.

> Romans 12:3

5 And when Jesus was entered into Capernaum, there came unto him a centurion, beseeching him,
6 And saying, Lord, my servant lieth at home sick of the palsy, grievously tormented.
7 And Jesus saith unto him, I will come and heal him.
8 The centurion answered and said, Lord, I am not worthy that thou shouldest come under my roof: but speak the word only, and my servant shall be healed.
9 For I am a man under authority, having soldiers under me: and I say to this man, Go, and he goeth; and to another, Come, and he cometh; and to my servant, Do this, and he doeth it.
10 When Jesus heard it, he marveled, and said to them that followed, Verily I say unto you, I have not found so great faith, no, not in Israel.

> Matthew 8:5-10

Wherefore, if God so clothe the grass of the field, which today is, and tomorrow is cast into the oven, shall he not much more clothe you, O ye of little faith?

> Matthew 6:30

And he saith unto them, Why are ye fearful, O ye of little faith? Then he arose, and rebuked the winds and the sea; and there was a great calm.

> Matthew 8:26

20 And Jesus said unto them, Because of your unbelief: for verily I say unto you, If ye have faith as a grain of mustard seed, ye shall say unto this mountain, Remove hence to yonder place; and it shall remove; and nothing shall be impossible unto you.

21 Howbeit this kind goeth not out but by prayer and fasting.

Matthew 17:20-21

38 And he was in the hinder part of the ship, asleep on a pillow: and they awake him, and say unto him, Master, carest thou not that we perish?
39 And he arose, and rebuked the wind, and said unto the sea, Peace, be still. And the wind ceased, and there was a great calm.
40 And he said unto them, Why are ye so fearful? how is it that ye have no faith?

Mark 4:38-40

5 And the apostles said unto the Lord, Increase our faith.
6 And the Lord said, If ye had faith as a grain of mustard seed, ye might say unto this sycamine tree, Be thou plucked up by the root, and be thou planted in the sea; and it should obey you.

Luke 17:5-6

Where is your faith?

Your faith is in your mouth. What you believe is what you speak, for out of the abundance of the heart the mouth speaks. I can know your faith level by just listening to what you speak. You need to guard your mouth until it comes into alignment with what the Word says.

The things in which you have faith are the things you are going to receive.

Sometimes that is not such a good thing, because that for which you have faith is the worst. This is the way the enemy gets you. You have to see the good things of God and quit looking at the things the enemy has surrounded you with to steal your faith, because that is his plan. He does not want you to realize that you have all power and authority on the earth. He wants you to believe he does. When he gets you to this point you begin to grow your faith, but in the wrong things.

> But what saith it? The word is nigh thee, even in thy mouth, and in thy heart: that is, the word of faith, which we preach;
>
> Romans 10:8

> And he said unto them, Where is your faith? And they being afraid wondered, saying one to another, What manner of man is this! for he commandeth even the winds and water, and they obey him.
>
> Luke 8:25

Faith brings those things you need.

You will never receive anything from God apart from faith. We see this very clearly in the Word.

> 6 But let him ask in faith, nothing wavering. For he that wavereth is like a wave of the sea driven with the wind and tossed.
> 7 For let not that man think that he shall receive any thing of the Lord.
>
> James 1:6-7

Wavering faith, that is, a lot of doubt mixed with trust in God, will keep you from receiving anything and everything God has to offer. You can't trust God in some things and not in others. That may work for you but it doesn't work for God. He calls you an unstable person and says that He will not give you anything. But we see that faith moves the heart of God, and when you stand in faith there is nothing that you cannot receive from God. I know that is a bold statement, but I didn't make it - God did; so do you believe Him???

Look at the scriptures below to see how God was moved by just seeing the faith of people. Some didn't even have to ask, but rather He did for them because He saw their faith.

> Then touched he their eyes, saying, According to your faith be it unto you.
>
> Matthew 9:29

1 James, a servant of God and of the Lord Jesus Christ, to the twelve tribes which are scattered abroad, greeting.
2 My brethren, count it all joy when ye fall into divers temptations;
3 Knowing this, that the trying of your faith worketh patience.
4 But let patience have her perfect work, that ye may be perfect and entire, wanting nothing.
5 If any of you lack wisdom, let him ask of God, that giveth to all men liberally, and upbraideth not; and it shall be given him.
6 But let him ask in faith, nothing wavering. For he that wavereth is like a wave of the sea driven with the wind and tossed.
7 For let not that man think that he shall receive any thing of the Lord.
8 A double minded man is unstable in all his ways.

James 1:1-8

And, behold, they brought to him a man sick of the palsy, lying on a bed: and Jesus seeing their faith said unto the sick of the palsy; Son, be of good cheer; thy sins be forgiven thee.

Matthew 9:2

27 And when Jesus departed thence, two blind men followed him, crying, and saying, Thou son of David, have mercy on us.
28 And when he was come into the house, the blind men came to him: and Jesus saith unto them, Believe ye that I am able to do this? They said unto him, Yea, Lord.
29 Then touched he their eyes, saying, According to your faith be it unto you.

Matthew 9:27-29

When Jesus saw their faith, he said unto the sick of the palsy, Son, thy sins be forgiven thee.

Mark 2:5

> And he said unto her, Daughter, thy faith hath made thee whole; go in peace, and be whole of thy plague.
>
> Mark 5:34

> And Jesus said unto him, Receive thy sight: thy faith hath saved thee.
>
> Luke 18:42

> The same heard Paul speak: who stedfastly beholding him, and perceiving that he had faith to be healed,
>
> Acts 14:9

Faith beyond prayer

We have been taught to connect faith and prayer, but let us look at how Jesus took faith beyond prayer and into the arena of works. In other words, He acted on the faith that He had as well as the faith that others had. James tells us that we can have faith, but if we never do anything with it we might as well not have it at all, because it is dead.

Interesting fact: Faith has life, because how can something die except first it is alive or has life? The thing that gives life to your faith is using it.

> But wilt thou know, O vain man, that faith without works is dead?
>
> James 2:20

> For as the body without the spirit is dead, so faith without works is dead also.
>
> James 2:26

15 Lord, have mercy on my son: for he is lunatic, and sore vexed: for ofttimes he falleth into the fire, and oft into the water.
16 And I brought him to thy disciples, and they could not cure him.
17 Then Jesus answered and said, O faithless and perverse generation, how long shall I be with you? how long shall I suffer you? bring him hither to me.
18 And Jesus rebuked the devil; and he departed out of him: and the child was cured from that very hour.
19 Then came the disciples to Jesus apart, and said, Why could not we cast him out?
20 And Jesus said unto them, Because of your unbelief: for verily I say unto you, If ye have faith as a grain of mustard seed, ye shall say unto this mountain, Remove hence to yonder place; and it shall remove; and nothing shall be impossible unto you.
21 Howbeit this kind goeth not out but by prayer and fasting.

Matthew 17:15-21

Justification

We need to first get the definition of the word justified. That is "to declare innocent or guiltless; absolve; acquit." We are not justified just because we know the Word or even because we do what the Word says and follow the law. We are only justified by the faith of Jesus. We have to work to attain the same faith that Jesus had. If it were not attainable, God would not have told us in Galatians 2:20, "and the life which I now live in the flesh I live by the faith of the Son of God, who loved me, and gave himself for me." We live in the flesh but we are to have the faith of God.

> 16 Knowing that a man is not justified by the works of the law, but by the faith of Jesus Christ, even we have believed in Jesus Christ, that we might be justified by the faith of Christ, and not by the works of the law: for by the works of the law shall no flesh be justified.
> 17 But if, while we seek to be justified by Christ, we ourselves also are found sinners, is therefore Christ the minister of sin? God forbid.

18 For if I build again the things which I destroyed, I make myself a transgressor.
19 For I through the law am dead to the law, that I might live unto God.
20 I am crucified with Christ: nevertheless I live; yet not I, but Christ liveth in me: and the life which I now live in the flesh I live by the faith of the Son of God, who loved me, and gave himself for me.
21 I do not frustrate the grace of God: for if righteousness come by the law, then Christ is dead in vain.

Galatians 2:16-21

How do we get faith?

Initially every man is dealt the measure of faith; this is your seed. Faith is then fed by hearing the word of God. Practically, we have learned that whatever we hear often enough is what we begin to believe. This is why we MUST let what we hear be based on the Word of God. If we are hearing the Word but not mixing it with faith, it will profit us nothing.

> For I say, through the grace given unto me, to every man that is among you, not to think of himself more highly than he ought to think; but to think soberly, according as God hath dealt to every man the measure of faith.
>
> Romans 12:3
>
> So then faith cometh by hearing, and hearing by the word of God.
>
> Romans 10:17
>
> For unto us was the gospel preached, as well as unto them: but the word preached did not profit them, not being mixed with faith in them that heard it.
>
> Hebrews 4:2

So you say, "How do I fit all of this together?" Let me bring it all together for you. God has given you a measure of faith. You then use that faith to receive Jesus as your Lord and Savior, because that has to be done through faith.

Next you get into the Word of God and begin to read it, but go beyond there; read it aloud. It is important that you hear what it says with your ears, not just see what it says with your eyes.

Now it is your responsibility to begin to do what it says. The more you hear and the more you do of what it says, the more you grow. Quit arguing with God and trying to tell Him that He doesn't mean what He says. HE MEANS EXACTLY WHAT HE SAYS, and He does not change just because the century changed.

For instance, He told women to dress modestly. Just because fashion changed, GOD DID NOT CHANGE OR CHANGE HIS MIND. Just DO IT!! You will find that your faith and trust in Him will grow beyond measure. But if you waiver by making excuses you will never get anything from God.

If you "run into a bump in the road" so to speak, then the Word says,"O.K, time for fasting and prayer to build your faith to get you beyond this point" (these are my words). So just do it. Fast, pray, DO IT and move on.

The Kingdom of God is always advancing, so you must never let the enemy hang you up. Just do what needs to be done, and the more you move forward the more your faith grows. Then God will say of you, "I have not seen so great a faith," just as He said of the centurion.

More than ever receiving anything from the Kingdom, our hearts desire should be to please the Father.

Chapter 18

Keys

Keys are the instruments by which doors are locked and unlocked. The keys of the kingdom are the principles, precepts, laws, and systems by which the kingdom functions. The keys must be learned and applied by the citizens in order to appropriate the benefits and privileges of the kingdom. These benefits and privileges are free but require a key to obtain.

> And I will give unto thee the keys of the kingdom of heaven: and whatsoever thou shalt bind on earth shall be bound in heaven: and whatsoever thou shalt loose on earth shall be loosed in heaven.
> Matthew 16:19

The text here indicates that bind and bound are used in the context to mean lock and unlock, because that is what keys are designed to do. Here are a few keys from the scriptures

> 14 Is any sick among you? let him call for the elders of the church; and let them pray over him, anointing him with oil in the name of the Lord:
> 15 And the prayer of faith shall save the sick, and the Lord shall raise him up; and if he have committed sins, they shall be forgiven him.
> James 5:14-15

In this scripture the key is calling for the elders of the church, then the elders praying and anointing with oil. This is one key that will unlock healing and forgiveness.

> Confess your faults one to another, and pray one for another, that ye may be healed. The effectual fervent prayer of a righteous man availeth much.
>
> James 5:16

Here the key is to confess your faults to one another, but in these days be careful to whom you confess them. Sadly, not everyone is trust-worthy nor is everyone in right standing with the King to be able to pray that fervent prayer. However, we see that this also unlocks a door to a different type of healing.

> Give, and it shall be given unto you; good measure, pressed down, and shaken together, and running over, shall men give into your bosom. For with the same measure that ye mete withal it shall be measured to you again.
>
> Luke 6:38

Here we see the key to receiving is giving. In so many cases, as you search for keys in the Kingdom, you will find that they are contrary to the ways of man.

As great as knowledge is of the Kingdom of God, the next most sought after information is, "What are the Keys?" The answer to this is very easy but the process of finding them takes much more time. So I am going to try to help you at least get started discovering the Keys. It is important that it be noted that all of these are keys OF the kingdom, but entrance to the Kingdom must come by discovering first the key TO the Kingdom. The key TO the Kingdom will be discussed in the next chapter.

We have been taught over and over that the scriptures are all about seed time and harvest. I believe that to be truly stated, but only to a minimal extent. The focus has been placed on this teaching in order to get people to support the work that a man or ministry has started. While the principle is good and right, the motivation is not. Not all soil is good soil and not all soil is ordained by God. You will need discernment to know where to sow.

The Word of God is a book of the law and is based on CONDITIONAL PROMISES. These conditional promises are all keys to unlock resources in the Kingdom of God. Some say, "What is a CONDITIONAL PROMISE?" Simply put, it is a promise that requires you to meet a condition to receive it. Seed time and harvest are a small part of this. You plant a seed, you get a harvest; you don't plant, you don't get anything. Thus the promises of God are there, but if you don't meet the condition you will not receive the promise. The KEYS OF THE KINGDOM are the conditions that you must meet to receive the promise.

Let me encourage you to search the scriptures for as many keys as you can find. The more keys you find the more resources you can unlock in the Kingdom. Just meet the condition and the promise is yours.

Chapter 19

Treason

Treason is the ultimate form of betrayal. It is an act of aligning oneself with the enemies of their government. In the Kingdom of God treason is committed when a citizen of the Kingdom falls into alliance with the kingdom of darkness (Satan) by submitting to the influence of that kingdom (sin).

When one commits treason the first thing that happens is that they lose all of their rights and privileges as a citizen, and any authority that may have been bestowed upon them is immediately removed. It works the same in the Kingdom of God; cooperating with any spirit that is not of God is called sin and is punishable by immediately losing your authority and position in the Kingdom.

Never under estimate the strategies of the enemy, and believe me he has many. He has no power except to get you to believe a lie (wiles). Once you believe the lie and act on it, you open a door for further activity in your life by the enemy of your God. Even though he has no power, he knows you and he develops a strategy, especially designed for you, based on your strengths and weaknesses. In His Word God gives us a way to protect ourselves from the temptation of this type of attack from the enemy.

> 10 Finally, my brethren, be strong in the Lord, and in the power of his might.
> 11 Put on the whole armour of God, that ye may be able to stand against the wiles of the devil.
> 12 For we wrestle not against flesh and blood, but against principalities, against powers, against the rulers of the

darkness of this world, against spiritual wickedness in high places.

13 Wherefore take unto you the whole armour of God, that ye may be able to withstand in the evil day, and having done all, to stand.

14 Stand therefore, having your loins girt about with truth, and having on the breastplate of righteousness;

15 And your feet shod with the preparation of the gospel of peace;

16 Above all, taking the shield of faith, wherewith ye shall be able to quench all the fiery darts of the wicked.

17 And take the helmet of salvation, and the sword of the Spirit, which is the word of God:

18 Praying always with all prayer and supplication in the Spirit, and watching thereunto with all perseverance and supplication for all saints.

Ephesians 6:10-18

Losing your authority

Treason results in the loss of authority. One of the main questions I am asked when teaching about the Kingdom of God is, "Why don't I have that authority?" I have put together a list from the Word that God says will cause you to lose your authority. These things will keep you from walking in authority, but the real reason is that you are committing treason against the government of God by your willful cooperation with a foreign government (the kingdom of darkness, "Satan") better known as SIN.

This can happen either knowingly or unknowingly because of ignorance. This is the one thing that God said in Hosea 4:6 would destroy his people.

> My people are destroyed for lack of knowledge; because you [the priestly nation] have rejected knowledge, I will also reject you that you shall be no priest to Me; seeing you have forgotten the law of your God, I will also forget your children.
>
> Hosea 4:6 (Amplified Bible)

Let's look at the Word of God for more examples.

> 16 This I say then, Walk in the Spirit, and ye shall not fulfill the lust of the flesh.
> 17 For the flesh lusteth against the Spirit, and the Spirit against the flesh: and these are contrary the one to the other: so that ye cannot do the things that ye would.
> 18 But if ye be led of the Spirit, ye are not under the law.
> 19 Now the works of the flesh are manifest, which are these; Adultery, fornication, uncleanness (anything that is unholy), lasciviousness (lewd or lustful)
> 20 Idolatry, witchcraft (any form of manipulation), hatred, variance (the fact or state of being in disagreement), emulations (envious rivalry), wrath, strife, seditions (insurrection against lawful authority), heresies (dissent or deviation from God's Word),
> 21 Envyings, murders, drunkenness, revellings (rebellions against God), and such like: of the which I tell you before, as I have also told you in time past, that they, which do such things, shall not inherit the Kingdom of God.
> 22 But the fruit of the Spirit is love, joy, peace, longsuffering, gentleness, goodness, faith,
> 23 Meekness, temperance: against such there is no law.
> 24 And they that are Christ's have crucified the flesh with the affections and lusts.
> 25 If we live in the Spirit, let us also walk in the Spirit.
> 26 Let us not be desirous of vain glory, provoking one another, envying one another.
>
> Galatians 5:16-26

This is a pretty good list of things but here are a few more from the Word.

> 9 Know ye not that the unrighteous shall not inherit the Kingdom of God? Be not deceived: neither fornicators, nor idolaters, nor adulterers, nor effeminate (having feminine qualities untypical of a man), nor abusers of themselves with mankind,
> 10 Nor thieves, nor covetous, nor drunkards, nor revilers (to use abusive language), nor extortioners (obtain from a

person by force, intimidation, or undue or illegal power), shall inherit the Kingdom of God.

I Corinthians 6:9 -10

This is God's list, not mine. I do, however, find it very interesting that all of the things He lists have one thing in common. They are all about you: what you want, what you think you need, and how things are going to affect you.

The Kingdom of God is about Him, not you. In order to inherit His Kingdom and operate in it with full authority, you MUST take on His nature and lay aside yours. He is a holy God, and He expects those who inherit His Kingdom to be like Him.

Because it is written, Be ye holy; for I am holy.

1 Peter 1:16

I want to make a list from the text above in order to make it easier for you to identify the things that you might have operating in your life. The first four deal with the aligning of oneself with a spirit of perversion. Once you open this door, it not only separates you from God but will lead you into even worse acts of perversion. Any type of sexual activity outside the God-ordained relationship of marriage between one man and one woman is based on your self-will and will separate you from God. This will cost you your position in the Kingdom and the loss of your authority.

Adultery- sexual relationship outside of the marriage

Fornication - sexual relationship between unmarried people

Abusers of themselves with mankind -perverted sexual acts with others

Effeminate - homosexual relationships

Uncleanness - any activity that is not "holy" before the Lord

Lasciviousness- lewd and lustful thoughts and activities

Idolatry - Placing anything or anyone before God. This can be a ball game, money, another person, etc. The thing that is your first priority is the thing that can become an idol in your heart.

Witchcraft - Any form of manipulation. This includes those times when you formulate in your mind the things you are going to say or do in order to get a desired reaction by manipulating a person or a situation.

Hatred - Should need no explanation. Extreme ungodly dislike for someone

Variance - Ungodly disagreements. Disagreeing with other and even with God about things that just don't matter

Emulations - Ungodly competition or rivalry

Wrath - Ungodly anger. If your anger is because of the way a particular thing affects you, then it is probably ungodly. Jesus got angry because of the way things affected the Kingdom of God.

Strife - Violent conflict. This can be spoken or unspoken and is an ungodly emotion.

Seditions - Taking an ungodly stand against lawful authority. (Oops, this one got me - rebellion against wearing a seat belt). Seditions are rooted in rebellion.

Heresies - Twisting the Word of God to suit your way of thinking and your situation.

Envying - A feeling of hatred and anger toward someone because of what they have or whom they are with. This also leads to covetousness, which means wanting something or someone that belongs to another person.

Murders - Taking the God-given life of a person

Drunkenness - A state of not having full control of yourself because of an excessive amount of anything, whether it is alcohol or drugs, legal or illegal. Today it is referred to as "getting high."

Revellings - Rebellion against God and the things of God. This includes His laws, commandments and statutes, and any other directions that we have been given by His Word.

Vain glory - Glory that we seek to feed our own ego. Everything in our lives should bring glory to God, not to ourselves.

Extortioners - Obtaining something from a person by force, intimidation, or undue or illegal power.

How did you come out after this list? I pray that if you found any of these things in your life, you stopped, repented and made the decision to change your ways. Not one thing on this list is worth being out of relationship with God.

...God is not a God of Compromise

Compromise is a demonic spirit. We can know this by the scripture in James.

> But above all things, my brethren, swear not, neither by heaven, neither by the earth, neither by any other oath: but let your yea be yea; and your nay, nay; lest ye fall into condemnation.
>
> James 5:12

> 6 But let him ask in faith, nothing wavering. For he that wavereth is like a wave of the sea driven with the wind and tossed.
> 7 For let not that man think that he shall receive any thing of the Lord.
> 8 A double minded man is unstable in all his ways.
>
> James 1:6-8

We see here that the ways of God are stable and sure. They are black and white with no gray areas. Wavering is compromise.

> So then because thou art lukewarm, and neither cold nor hot, I will spue thee out of my mouth.
>
> Revelation 3:16

In the eyes of God lukewarm is the same as being cold, or that is to say, being in the kingdom of darkness. The Kingdom of God and the kingdom of darkness are very defined. You are either of your Father God or of your father the devil. Do not be deceived; there is no middle ground. We can see the stand that God Himself has taken on this issue.

> Sanctify yourselves therefore, and be ye holy: for I am the LORD your God.
> Leviticus 20:7

> But as he which hath called you is holy, so be ye holy in all manner of conversation;
> 1 Peter 1:15

> Because it is written, Be ye holy; for I am holy.
> 1 Peter 1:16

God's expectation of us is "holiness." Recently I read a true statement that all words have a definition, so let's look at the definition of holiness: not man's, but God' s.

> According as he hath chosen us in him before the foundation of the world, that we should be holy and without blame before him in love:
> Ephesians 1:4

> That he might present it to himself a glorious church, not having spot, or wrinkle, or any such thing; but that it should be holy and without blemish.
> Ephesians 5:27

To be holy is to stand blameless before God. If you stand before God thinking he will accept your excuses for the sin in your life, you need to think again. He made provision through His Son that you might walk blameless before Him. He will not accept turning your back on God. Remember, you may allow the devil to tempt you to fall into deception, but God is not fooled. Now let's go a step farther.

Darkness and light cannot be present at the same time. Either there is light or there is darkness.

> I am come a light into the world, that whosoever believeth on me should not abide in darkness.
>
> John 12:46

> The night is far spent, the day is at hand: let us therefore cast off the works of darkness, and let us put on the armour of light.
>
> Romans 13:12

> Be ye not unequally yoked together with unbelievers: for what fellowship hath righteousness with unrighteousness? And what communion hath light with darkness?
>
> 2 Corinthians 6:14

> But ye are a chosen generation, a royal priesthood, an holy nation, a peculiar people; that ye should shew forth the praises of him who hath called you out of darkness into his marvellous light;
>
> 1 Peter 2:9

> This then is the message which we have heard of him, and declare unto you, that God is light, and in him is no darkness at all.
>
> 1 John 1:5

> The light of the body is the eye: therefore when thine eye is single, thy whole body also is full of light; but when thine eye is evil, thy body also is full of darkness.
>
> Luke 11:34

God warns us that we need to know the Word and have a relationship with Him. If not, then all we can have in our lives is darkness. That is the only revelation we have of what is right or wrong.

> Take heed therefore that the light which is in thee be not darkness.
> Luke 11:35

Many people have asked me why they cannot receive the Baptism of the Holy Spirit. They have tried on so many occasions, and in many cases have given up. I can only find two reasons, so I want to talk about them.

The first is their expectation of what the in-filling of the Holy Spirit really is. Some immediately begin to speak with tongues as the Spirit gives utterance; others do not. Is one less filled than the other? The answer is no. However, the one who does not eventually will, because it is a characteristic of the nature of the Holy Spirit. The most visible sign is a change in the life of a person.

You cannot be filled with the Spirit of God and not change. Every time you enter His presence you will change a little more. The expectation of an immediate vocal manifestation does, however, cause some to think they have not received, when in fact they have. They continue to seek for the Baptism of the Holy Spirit when they should be asking for the evidence to manifest in their lives.

I also want to note here that speaking in tongues does not mean a person is filled with the Spirit of God. I will address that a little later.

The second reason some are not filled is found in the preceding scripture.

God will not place His Spirit in an unholy vessel.

> Be ye not unequally yoked together with unbelievers: for what fellowship hath righteousness with unrighteousness? And what communion hath light with darkness?
> 2 Corinthians 6:14

Many are standing before God with all forms of sin in their lives and asking to be filled with His Spirit. Sorry, this is never going to happen. HOWEVER, and this is very important, Satan has a counterfeit for the things of God including the Holy Spirit. This has over the years given lots of people a false sense of security. That is the intent of Satan. You will not seek what you think you have.

PLUS, being able to continue in your sin and then spout out words that sound like the Holy Spirit cause many to validate the sin in their lives, thinking that God is using them, so they must be O.K. That, my friend, is exactly what Satan would have you believe. A good rule of thumb would be, "If there is SIN involved it cannot be God."

So here is my advice to each of you.

You want to receive the Holy Spirit? **Get right with God**

You want to walk in power and authority? **Get right with God**

You want to walk in righteousness? **Get right with God**

You want to live a blameless and sin free life? **Get right with God**

So how do you "Get right with God?"

Quit playing games, quit walking after and satisfying the flesh, repent and turn from the wickedness in your life. Remember, God knows your heart, so He knows if you are playing games. **Just GET REAL**.

Chapter 20

Ruling the Visible from the Invisible

This is what the Kingdom of God is all about. Satan has been doing this throughout all of history, but we as the body of Christ have made it almost taboo. I hear too often spoken by Christians, "What will be will be," or,"God has it all under control," or, "That's just the way it is," and the list goes on and on. The truth is that some Christians are ignorant when it comes to the things of the Spirit, and it is easier to do nothing than to do something.

We have become so caught up in the distractions in our own lives that we forget that God created us for a purpose. We need to get with God's program and on His agenda, setting our own selfish agenda aside, if we are to see the coming of the King and the establishment of His Kingdom.

I was just reminded of our troops on the battlefield. When they signed on with a branch of the armed forces, they gave up their rights to allow their personal lives to supersede their service to the United States and its purposes. If the government says, "Go," they cannot say, "No, I have things I need to do." They MUST set everything aside for the purposes of the government. They leave home, family and friends for a greater purpose which they agreed to serve.

Our government is far greater and has a much greater purpose on this earth. Those who SAY they have joined with the government of God, (that is, the Kingdom of God), to see His purposes established, tend to put everything ahead of Him, and if there is any time left they will give that time to God.

> 56 For the Son of man is not come to destroy men's lives, but to save them. And they went to another village.
> 57 And it came to pass, that, as they went in the way, a certain man said unto him, Lord, I will follow thee whithersoever thou goest.
> 58 And Jesus said unto him, Foxes have holes, and birds of the air have nests; but the Son of man hath not where to lay his head.
> 59 And he said unto another, Follow me. But he said, Lord, suffer me first to go and bury my father.
> 60 Jesus said unto him, Let the dead bury their dead: but go thou and preach the kingdom of God.
> 61 And another also said, Lord, I will follow thee; but let me first go bid them farewell, which are at home at my house.
> 62 And Jesus said unto him, No man, having put his hand to the plough, and looking back, is fit for the kingdom of God.
>
> Luke 9:56-62

In the Kingdom of God nothing can come ahead of Him. People sign on with the Kingdom of God every day. Unfortunately, they do not receive authority just by signing on. This is a deception that some have been led to believe. I want to first lay out the process so that you can understand it.

You must be "born again."

> 1 There was a man of the Pharisees, named Nicodemus, a ruler of the Jews:
> 2 The same came to Jesus by night, and said unto him, Rabbi, we know that thou art a teacher come from God: for no man can do these miracles that thou doest, except God be with him.
> 3 Jesus answered and said unto him, Verily, verily, I say unto thee, Except a man be born again, he cannot see the kingdom of God.

> 4 Nicodemus saith unto him, How can a man be born when he is old? can he enter the second time into his mother's womb, and be born?
> 5 Jesus answered, Verily, verily, I say unto thee, Except a man be born of water and of the Spirit, he cannot enter into the kingdom of God.
> 6 That which is born of the flesh is flesh; and that which is born of the Spirit is spirit.
> 7 Marvel not that I said unto thee, Ye must be born again.
>
> John 3:1-7

In this passage Jesus made it as plain as it can be made. First you were born into this world through your mother's womb, "born of water" and "born of flesh." Now you MUST BE **"BORN OF THE SPIRIT."**

Being born of the "Spirit" is a two-fold process. The first is Salvation.

Salvation is made up of two parts: acceptance and righteousness.

The first part is acceptance- we must accept and confess Jesus Christ as the Son of God and His resurrection.

> 9 That if thou shalt confess with thy mouth the Lord Jesus, and shalt believe in thine heart that God hath raised him from the dead, thou shalt be saved.
> 10 For with the heart man believeth unto righteousness; and with the mouth confession is made unto salvation.
>
> Romans 10:9-10

Even here we see another two-part process - righteousness and salvation. Salvation does not stand alone. The next scripture tells us that man can say a lot of things, but if you listen long enough they will reveal what is truly in their hearts.

> O generation of vipers, how can ye, being evil, speak good things? for out of the abundance of the heart the mouth speaketh.
>
> Matthew 12:34

Righteousness or "right standing"

There are things that we must do ourselves to come into a position of right standing with God the Father. One of the most important is forgiveness, that being our forgiving others, not just our being forgiven.

> 14 For if ye forgive men their trespasses, your heavenly Father will also forgive you:
> 15 But if ye forgive not men their trespasses, neither will your Father forgive your trespasses.
>
> Matthew 6:14-15

Well, that is plain enough. To be in right standing with the Father you must be in a state of constant forgiveness. I find it interesting that the last temptation of Christ on the cross was unforgiveness. That is why He said, "Father, forgive them: for they know not what they do."

> Then said Jesus, Father, forgive them; for they know not what they do. And they parted his raiment, and cast lots.
>
> Luke 23:34

Accepting Jesus as the Son of God and forgiving others brings us into a position in the Kingdom with the Father to receive that which He has for us. David found the secret to staying in that position of right standing as he prayed.

> Let the words of my mouth, and the meditation of my heart, be acceptable in thy sight, O LORD, my strength, and my redeemer.
>
> Psalm 19:14

This is the key to remaining in right standing. Guard your heart, your mind and your mouth.

Since you have come this far, we can talk about Kingdom authority, which is necessary if you are to rule the seen from the unseen.

There is another step that MUST be taken to operate in the POWER and authority of the Kingdom of God. Let's go to the scriptures to find this.

> But ye shall receive power, after that the Holy Ghost is come upon you: and ye shall be witnesses unto me both in Jerusalem, and in all Judaea, and in Samaria, and unto the uttermost part of the earth.
>
> Acts 1:8

> How God anointed Jesus of Nazareth with the Holy Ghost and with power: who went about doing good, and healing all that were oppressed of the devil; for God was with him.
>
> Acts 10:38

> I indeed baptize you with water unto repentance, but he that cometh after me is mightier than I, whose shoes I am not worthy to bear: He shall baptize you with the Holy Ghost, and with fire:
>
> Matthew 3:11

> And I knew him not: but he that sent me to baptize with water, the same said unto me, Upon whom thou shalt see the Spirit descending, and remaining on him, the same is he which baptizeth with the Holy Ghost.
>
> John 1:33

It was the power of His authority that the people of that day were so amazed by. It was that power that was a witness of who He was. This power only comes through being baptized in the Holy Spirit.

> And they were astonished at his doctrine: for his word was with power.
>
> Luke 4:32

We go on into the scriptures to find that Jesus gave that same power and authority to those who were His disciples and had been BAPTIZED with the Holy Ghost (John 1:33).

> Behold, I give unto you power to tread on serpents and scorpions, and over all the power of the enemy: and nothing shall by any means hurt you.
>
> Luke 10:19

> Then he called his twelve disciples together, and gave them power and authority over all devils, and to cure diseases.
>
> Luke 9:1

Many say, "That was for the disciples," and they are correct. They just don't seem to know the definition of a disciple.

A disciple is a follower and student of a mentor, teacher, or otherwise figure. We know that He was not just talking to the twelve disciples, also called apostles. As we read further we find that Jesus was not the only one who had disciples. Here we find mention of John's disciples and disciples of the Pharisees.

> And they said unto him, Why do the disciples of John fast often, and make prayers, and likewise the disciples of the Pharisees; but thine eat and drink?
>
> Luke 5:33

> When therefore the Lord knew how the Pharisees had heard that Jesus made and baptized more disciples than John,
>
> John 4:1

In Luke we find that Jesus had many more than twelve disciples because it refers to a multitude of disciples.

> And when he was come nigh, even now at the descent of the mount of Olives, the whole multitude of the disciples began to rejoice and praise God with a loud voice for all the mighty works that they had seen.
>
> Luke 19:37

In John 8 Jesus tells how you become a disciple of His.

> Then said Jesus to those Jews which believed on him, If ye continue in my word, then are ye my disciples indeed;
>
> John 8:31

It is the sole intent of a disciple to follow after the one that is disciplining him. If you do not love someone you will not follow them.

Let's look at how we know that we love God.

> He that hath my commandments, and keepeth them, he it is that loveth me: and he that loveth me shall be loved of my Father, and I will love him, and will manifest myself to him.
>
> John 14:21

So we see that complete power and authority is given to disciples of Jesus (Luke 9:1, Luke 10:19, etc)

Let's stop here and sum up where we are:

1. We have accepted Jesus as the Son of God.

2. We have forgiven others and constantly continue to forgive others.

3. We have been baptized in the Holy Ghost and have received power.

4. We have become disciples of Christ and keep His commandments.

5. We are in right standing with the Kingdom of God based on our commitment to love God and keep His commandments.

Now we are ready to walk in authority and power of the Kingdom of God. Thus we have positioned ourselves to change the visible from the realm of the invisible. But, BEWARE, your total commitment is to always be,

"Not my will, but Thine be done."

Now to proceed forward, you need to stay in constant communion with the Father, the Son and especially your closet friend, the Holy Spirit. Learn when to pray and when to speak with authority. Begin to exercise your authority in a realm that goes beyond prayer. Let the kingdom of darkness know who you are and that you are now in control. Let's push back the kingdom of darkness and establish the throne of God here on earth.

"Let's take back what Adam gave away."

Our Dominion Authority

Welcome to the realm of the Spirit and the Kingdom of God.

Chapter 21

The Glory of God

The Glory of God is very simple to define. Just as the Holy Spirit is the essence of the presence of the Father and the Son on the earth so also the Glory is the natural manifestation of that presence. I find that those trying to explain the Glory of God are too often just trying to explain the manifestations. We need to take our focus off of the manifestations and put our focus on Him.

If you are filled with the Holy Spirit then you are filled with His Glory because He and His Glory are one. Where you go He goes and the more time you spend in His presence the more of Him you will see manifest around you.

> 10 And it came to pass, when the priests were come out of the holy place, that the cloud filled the house of the Lord,
> 11 So that the priests could not stand to minister because of the cloud: for the glory of the Lord had filled the house of the Lord.
>
> 1 Kings 8:10-11

We see the priests, in their place set apart for communion with God, coming forth filled with his presence and then we see the manifestation of His presence. The manifestation of His presence should be an everyday normal occurrence in your life when you spend time with Him. Sadly, it is so rare in the lives of most that when they see it they are astounded, shocked and totally surprised. Living in the manifestation of the Glory of God should be our everyday lifestyle. Books are written and doctrines are formed to try to explain what should be normal, but because we fail to spend time with Him we are trying to find a short cut to the Glory.

There is no shortcut my friend. It takes sacrifice of your time and energy to be in His presence. You may for a short time enjoy the benefits of the manifestation in someone else's life that has made the sacrifice but how much better to have it operate in your life.

My daily life is totally filled with what some call the "supernatural" but for me it is the normal everyday lifestyle that I live. When I start relating some of the things that happen at times people just stare in awe but I do not relate to those things that way. They are occurrences that happen because I have learned to spend time in His presence and operate my life according to His Kingdom principles. For me they are as normal as driving a car, or cooking a meal.

Everything that you will ever need is contained in the Holy Spirit and if He lives within you then you already have what you need it is just a matter of your faith causing it to manifest into the realm of the seen, regardless of what it is you need.

I encourage you to seek Him and His Kingdom and then you WILL see His Glory. Seek the source of the manifestation not the manifestation.

Made in the USA
Charleston, SC
28 August 2013